JESUS at the HEART of LIFE
The Spirituality of Being Human

JESUS at the HEART of LIFE
The Spirituality of Being Human

Nicholas Lohkamp, O.F.M.

ST.
ANTHONY
MESSENGER
PRESS

CINCINNATI, OHIO

Cover and book design by June Pfaff
ISBN 0-86716-225-2
Published by St. Anthony Messenger Press
Printed in the U.S.A.

Contents

Introduction

Why a book on incarnational spirituality? When I tell people about it, they often ask, "What do you mean by *incarnational spirituality*? It seems so abstract! Unreal!"

Let me put it this way. Jesus is the "Word-made-flesh." Jesus became fully human, entered fully into our human condition. Jesus became like us in all things but sin. Why?

Jesus affirms our humanness, shows us the meaning of being human, shows us the way to God. Jesus is our way. He leads us in the way to holiness, not in spite of our humanness, not by denying our humanness, but precisely in and through the graceful living of our human lives.

We can find meaning, and, what is more, we can find divine meaning in our daily lives. In our experience we discover Jesus. Precisely as human persons we are graced by God. In the ordinary events of daily life Jesus is present, calling us to follow him, calling us to share divine life in and through our experience.

I am convinced that Jesus is at the heart of every person's life: every personal relationship, every family and social experience, every human event, every human experience. In every moment, Jesus calls, "Follow me." That is the meaning of incarnational spirituality. That is what this little book is about.

The greatest obstacle to incarnational spirituality, however, is that most people seem to find it very difficult to believe that the ordinary affairs of daily life have a spiritual dimension. The fact that Jesus became flesh does not seem to make much difference.

In my own experience of trying to live a spiritual life for the past sixty-seven years, I have had great difficulty accepting myself and finding Jesus in my human experience. I ran into all sorts of obstacles. In many hidden ways I did not accept myself.

I also came to realize that other people found it hard to accept themselves and their human condition. As teacher, preacher, formation director and spiritual director, I was amazed to find that almost everyone was struggling to find God in their lives.

They would put it in different ways: "I just don't know how to pray"; "I don't feel good about myself"; "How can God really love me?"; "I feel my life is so dull and boring"; "Sometimes I want to throw in the towel; nothing seems to mean anything"; "I never have time for spiritual things."

Many people have encouraged me to write this book about incarnational spirituality. What I'm writing is the story of my life. It is the story of my own struggle to grow and develop in accepting myself, my humanity, my human condition. I have sought doggedly, often blindly, always painfully, yet ever hopefully, to become human, and so to follow Jesus. Everyone, I think, has a similar story.

Obviously, my story has its differences. I spent years in a seminary. I am a Franciscan and a priest. I lived my adult life in a religious community rather than in a more common setting. My friends tell me that I am an intense person in all that I do. But while your life-style and experiences are different from mine and while you may have grown up with a different spirituality (maybe after Vatican II), I write with the hope that you can identify to a greater or lesser degree with some of my struggles and insights. I hope that my story may help you understand yours.

The struggle to become human (and holy) takes many forms and shapes. It means appreciating my body in a balanced way. It involves believing in the goodness of my five senses. It includes coming to accept that I have feelings (some very powerful ones!). It includes daring to accept my sexuality as a powerful force for good in my life.

It means believing in myself, that I can be imaginative, fantasize, become somewhat creative (even in my sixties!). It means living intelligently and freely. Most of all it means trying to relate in healthy and loving ways to others. The struggle to become human has many fronts, all important. I would like to consider some of these in light of my story.

In the past forty years I've been in touch with many, many people—in classroom, confessional, parlor, lecture hall. When these people shared a bit of their lives with me, I found that we were on similar journeys—seeking God in our daily human experience. That is the way of incarnational spirituality.

My hope is that these reflections on my story will confirm the insights and struggles of others. I want to encourage others to dare to become more human. I am convinced that the best way to become better Christians is to become more human.

CHAPTER ONE

It's OK to Be Human!

Abe was in deep agony when I knew him. He had recently
married and his lovely wife, Sarah, was quickly pregnant—
with twins, as it turned out. Abe and Sarah were wondrously
happy, expecting. The night before she was due to give birth,
Sarah died suddenly. (Her death, it was discovered later, was
due to a uterine embolism.) Before the emergency squad
arrived, the twin girls were also dead.

Abe was utterly devastated. For months and months he was
lost. He felt so dead inside; his life was darkness. One day, as
we were talking, he cried out: "I went to Catholic school for so
many years. They taught us all the things we were *not* supposed
to do; they didn't teach us how to live! Why couldn't they teach
us what we were supposed to *do*, how we were supposed to *live*,
how to deal with this kind of tragedy?"

It was a cry of desperation. Yet, it was also a cry of the
human heart for a way of living that is real, that is rooted in the
human condition, that enables us to deal more positively with
the "stuff" of daily life, including tragedies, in a way that is
both human and faith-filled. A recent book by Wilkie Au, S.J.,
entitled *By Way of the Heart*, hits the nail on the head:

> To go to God by way of the heart is to take a path to
> holiness that is both graceful and human. It is graceful—
> not strained even in the midst of struggle—because it
> relies radically on the enabling power of God to achieve
> its end. While Christian transformation calls for personal
> responsibility and effort, it can only come about when
> God replaces our often cold hearts of stone with warm
> hearts of flesh capable of loving. The way of the heart is

also very human because it requires the involvement of the whole self—body and spirit, mind and emotions. The term "heart" is a traditional image for a way of perceiving, feeling, and loving that engages the total person.

Where We Come From

Like Abe, I wish I could have been educated more in how to live and less on how not to live. I wish my upbringing and education could have touched my heart and brought me to grips with the task of becoming human.

Would that I somehow could have experienced the promise of God found in Ezekiel: "I will give you a new heart and place a new spirit within you, taking from your bodies your stony hearts and giving you natural hearts" (Ezekiel 36:26).

I wish my initiation into the spiritual life had challenged me to accept rather than avoid or even deny the human. But such wishes are empty. That's not the way it was. Thank God, it's never too late to begin!

Some years ago a group of retreatants were discussing their understanding of "spirituality." One lady spoke rather bluntly: "I could never understand why spirituality had to be so negative and so inhuman!" I think she voiced something that resonated strongly the feelings of everyone present.

That was my experience of the "spirituality" I had learned. It seemed so confusing and unattractive. It entailed a lot of denial and rejection. The world of the "spiritual" was identified with the soul and the "other world." Spirituality meant doing certain kinds of things, such as going to church, obeying the law, praying the rosary.

Being "holy" meant giving up so much that excited me and ignited my curiosity. It seemed to imply that the body, senses, feelings, sexuality involved all kinds of dangers and juicy temptations! The human was very attractive, but so often out of bounds if you really wanted to be holy.

I felt divided. Religion and real life seemed unconnected. My time and energy, my preoccupations, likes and dislikes, sadness and joys, hopes and dreams—everything seemed caught up in and absorbed by my daily life of work, play, study, sports. Yet this was "secular" stuff, "profane," not really "spiritual."

Religion, the "spiritual," seemed to have little to do with daily life. The spiritual life seemed relegated to relatively rare moments and activities ("spiritual exercises") and took place in "sacred" places (church).

One day a man told me he had just made a weekend retreat. He found it to be a wonderful experience and came away feeling great. But he wondered what it had to do with his real life. "Everything seemed so far removed from my daily life," he said.

Again, that was my experience when I was young. Most of my life seemed doomed to be worthless for heaven, unimportant to God. Of course we were taught to make the "good intention," to recite the Morning Offering. But if most of my daily activity was not really "religious" or "spiritual," how was a good intention going to change the stripes?

I went to a high school seminary. I was supposed to be interested in "the spiritual." But I wasn't! Sports were much more exciting. I much preferred to go to the baseball field than to chapel. My batting average was more important than "steps to holiness."

In the novitiate this division between the spiritual and the human became more evident. Our novice master hardly ever smiled. But I was seventeen years old, and I didn't get very excited about it. I just went along with what I was told and what was expected of me.

I remember not blinking an eye when we were told not to smell flowers, not to hold babies in our arms. (I wasn't interested in flowers anyway, and babies were nowhere around!)

We Franciscans used a Benedictine book called *Tyrocinium*, and it stressed that the five senses could easily lead us astray, mostly, of course, into sins of impurity (at least that's what I imagined, which only made it come true). We were to keep our eyes downcast, not look at people. We were not to touch (much less kiss or hug). We were not to be concerned with how our food tasted. Now, that's nonincarnational spirituality! It's inhuman.

As I got older, I found out that my experience in the seminary was different from that of other high school kids, but they were not taught to appreciate the human either. They, too, were taught a spirituality divorced from the human.

Most everyone somehow got the impression: Watch out for your senses, such as looking (pictures and magazines). Watch out especially for the sense of touch. That leads into the area of "sex," and that's a big no-no! There were a lot of rules about what to avoid, a lot of emphasis on "don'ts."

In the seminary friendship was a big problem. Any close relationship was "bad." (Ordinary high school students were warned only about "bad companions.") I remember being told the danger of getting "too close" to anyone! Particular friendship was a "no-no." I didn't know what "a particular friendship" was, but the implications seemed clear: no friends! I grew to mistrust myself and became suspicious of others. That is what happens when the "spiritual" is separated from the human. It's not OK to be human.

Sexuality offers a glaring example of this kind of spirituality that avoids the human. Like most teenagers in my day, I received no instruction on sexuality, and I was afraid to ask any questions. I lived through the early and mid-teens in great ignorance, some fear and a lot of guilt. Sex was quite a burden (but also mysterious and exciting). I felt sure I was going to hell but didn't quite know why. I longed for some help, but none was offered, and I was afraid to ask.

When I was about eighteen, I finally did get some instruction on sexuality, but it was meager, simple and negative: "Don't do it" ("it" meant masturbation, and even worse, homosexual genital behavior).

This lack of instruction, either at home or in school, was a common experience of teenagers in the forties and fifties. What little instruction was given was negative and only gave rise to greater confusion, more unanswered questions and a lot of fear. No wonder we didn't learn the positive meaning of purity.

Our whole approach to life, to spirituality, seemed quite negative, even inhuman—not very incarnational!

A Harmful Spirituality

When we separate the human and the spiritual, when we imply that we can become holy without respecting our humanness, we are in some way denying that Jesus came in the flesh. Such spirituality is not healthy.

First, we don't appreciate very much the goodness and beauty of being human. We tend not to appreciate human love relationships, human closeness.

Second, we don't appreciate the importance of human history as salvation history. We miss the sacramental character of all reality, as seen in light of the Incarnation. We don't appreciate the sacramental character of our life in the Church, and the seven sacraments become separate and disconnected actions.

We tend to minimize or ignore the limitations and weakness of our human condition and fall into "perfectionism." We are inclined to exaggerate the evil in our actions, while minimizing the evil and sinfulness in our hearts, in our relations, in our society's systems and institutions.

Third, we find it so hard to accept ourselves in a holistic way: bodily as well as spiritual, sensual and emotional as well as intellectual and volitional, imaginative and remembering as well as sexual and creative.

Fourth, we tend to think we can earn God's love by our good works in obedience to laws. Forgiveness and heaven have to be earned. We become individualistic, wrapped in our own concerns and needs. We tend to become pessimistic, gloomy, even scrupulous. We become preoccupied with avoiding evil rather than enthusiastic in doing good.

Finally, we are divided into "parts." The religious, the sacred, the spiritual, become limited and narrow. The stuff of daily life, our ordinary work, endeavors, activities, are outside the parameters of the "spiritual." Most of our life, energy, activity, is mundane, ordinary, boring, unimportant, especially to God.

We need a spirituality that is human, healthy and whole.

A Spirituality That Is Human

Jesus taught us to find our way to God precisely in and through our human experience. We are called to share divine life precisely as human persons. Our human life and our spiritual life are one and the same. To separate them is detrimental, even destructive. Grace transforms the human; it does not destroy it.

Our hearts are human hearts, and God has promised to make a new covenant with us, in Jesus, by changing our stony hearts into hearts of flesh, hearts like the hearts of Jesus and Mary, hearts fully human, but also full of grace.

Today, many are speaking of the need for a true *lay* spirituality. For too long "lay spirituality" was but a diluted, watered-down version of "religious spirituality," or "priestly spirituality." Spiritual exercises for priests and religious were loaded on the laity, as though that were the only way, form and shape of becoming holy. For example, the whole approach to prayer and contemplation, which may work for priests and religious, does not work for the laity. Laypeople's daily situation is vastly different.

But, before we talk of "lay" spirituality (or "religious" or "priestly" or "masculine" or "feminine" spirituality), or any kind of spirituality, we need to notice the distinction between the deep, basic meaning of spirituality (which is common to all) and the more concrete expressions of spirituality.

The concrete expressions can be quite different. It is necessary, however, that these various concrete forms (lay, religious, clerical; Franciscan, Jesuit, Benedictine, etc.) be rooted in the same deep mystery of grace: the experience of God in human reality.

It seems to me we can make a double mistake in our approach to spirituality. First, we erroneously think we can simply adapt or modify the concrete expressions from one distinct group of people to another (for example, from clerical to lay). It just doesn't work.

Second, and even worse, we can mistakenly think that a spirituality that is "otherworldly, nonsecular, nonprofane, nonhuman" is good for anyone, including priests and religious.

Any form of spirituality that rejects what is truly human is not Christian. Any spirituality that does not welcome the human as mediating the divine is not true to the incarnation of Jesus or the sacramental aspect of all reality.

So, all people need a spirituality that fits who they are and the circumstances of their daily lives. This applies to all aspects of life: work, prayer, leisure, sexuality, marriage, family, politics, economics, etc.

Spirituality has to do with the depth of the human person. It also has to do with the breadth of the human person, every facet of life.

First, let's examine the depth. We need to go beneath and beyond the outward and more perceptible aspects of actions and behavior. We need to enter into the deeper and more mysterious level of valuing and personal priorities. Most of all we need to attend to the inmost depth and core of the person, the level of the heart. We will explore these depths in some detail later in Chapter Four.

Next, let's look at the breadth. The spiritual life of any person involves all aspects of his or her humanness: conditions, experiences, family relations and so on.

We believe that Jesus became human to save us from our sins, not from our humanness. Our life in Christ should challenge us to enter into our *humanness* and open our hearts and lives to the divine grace of the Spirit. Our life in the Spirit should call us to respond to grace in a human way, to become sons and daughters of God, precisely as human persons.

Some Dangers

There are those who become concerned when we speak of incarnational spirituality. They say we will so stress the human that we will overlook the divine, that we will turn spirituality into merely a psychological and therapeutic concern.

John M. Lozano, in *Grace and Brokenness in God's Country*, writes:

Isn't there a hidden danger here? Of course. The same danger that is latent in every christology: to stress one dimension (the divine) or the other (the human) in such a way that the incarnation would cease to be what it is. But we should note that this danger is inherent not only in a spirituality that stresses the human (non-transcendent) but also in one that stresses the divine (transcendent) dimension of Christ.

The truth is not to be found, I believe, when we separate and divide these aspects of spirituality. Rather, the truth lies in the union of the two: divine and human, secular and sacred, immanent and transcendent, nature and grace. That, I believe, is the mystery of Jesus, the Divine Word become human. That is the meaning of the Incarnation.

Likewise, psychology has much to offer us concerning personal and social dynamics. Spirituality is more than psychology, but we still depend on psychology to understand how spirituality affects us as humans.

Some of us Catholics seem to lack a deep sense of joy in our lives, a sense of mystery, a sense of enthusiasm in daily living. We don't seem to believe that God is in the human, that it's OK to be human. There is meaning and mystery in the most ordinary moment because Jesus is present in the human and the human is present in Jesus.

"The time is now. The Reign of God is here. You must change your minds and hearts, and believe in the Good News" (see Mark 1:15).

Things to Come

I wish to deal with spirituality by looking at some aspects that influenced my own development and the way I relate to others. My sense of myself (Chapter Three) will deeply influence the way I understand and feel about others, and the way I relate to them.

Obviously, for example, if I reject some aspects of myself, I'll have difficulty accepting others. If I resent or refuse to admit my own vulnerability and seek always to build my defenses, I'll see others as threatening and not relate comfortably to them.

However, in considering these various facets of my life, I want to be aware of the mystery and depth of my being. I want to look at the various aspects of my life in relation to my depth as a person (Chapter Four).

I want to glimpse the wondrous riches and facets of this depth and wholeness. This deep mystery of my life in relation to others, and so to God, is marvelously expressed and revealed outwardly through my body, its senses, feelings, sexuality (Chapter Five).

I'll also look at my spiritual life as a life of relationships (Chapter Six). It is in and through relating to others that I come closer to people, and so to God. Good, healthy, constructive relationships enflesh, and promote growth in, the spiritual life.

I want also to reflect on the meaning and importance of my vulnerability. This aspect has much to do with the way I feel about myself, the way I relate to others, the way I relate to Jesus. Vulnerability opens me to pain, suffering, sickness and ultimately to death (Chapter Seven).

CHAPTER TWO

'Who Do You Say I Am?'

Many elements, many aspects, many experiences, are involved in shaping our attitude toward life. Basic to a Christian's approach to life is what he or she feels about Jesus.

In Matthew 16:15 Jesus puts the question that is at the heart of a Christian's attitude toward life and spirituality: "But who do you say that I am?" Who is Jesus to me? How will Jesus shape my understanding of the spiritual life? Who Jesus is to me will determine my outlook on myself, my world, my life.

Who Jesus is to me will shape the way I relate to my husband or wife, family, coworkers, neighbors. Who Jesus is to me guides me in my work, my worries and concerns, my attitude toward material goods, education, beauty, health, life and death. "Who do *you* say I am?"

This is a very personal question. We can walk away from a lot of things, but it's hard to ignore this question if we want to live a Christian life.

It's a question that is not satisfied by a theoretical, heady answer. The question goes to the heart and involves my whole self. "Who do *you* say I am?" Who is Jesus to me?

For years I did not realize how important this question is. I spent four years in a Franciscan high school seminary, a year in the novitiate, four years in college and four more years studying theology, and in all these years this question did not really hit me where I lived, in my guts, in my heart.

I am appalled that I had such a meager and impersonal knowledge of Jesus after twenty-three years in Catholic schools. Only years later, when I began to struggle to accept my humanness, did I discover Jesus in new ways, and his question struck me dead-center.

My experience seems to be a striking example of what is rather common to most people. Most of us know quite a lot *about* Jesus, from home, Church, school. But the impact of Jesus in our lives seems to be rather weak.

To know about Jesus is not the same as knowing Jesus. To study, to learn about Jesus can result in lots of information, intellectual awareness, ability to answer theoretical questions about Jesus. But what's in the head is not necessarily in the heart. What's in the head does not necessarily translate into values, priorities, choices and behavior. I can know about Jesus and live an unchristian life. I can know about Jesus and yet he makes little difference in my attitude toward life.

Much later in life I began to appreciate the questions of the saints: "Oh God, who are you? Oh God, who am I?" Still later it began to dawn on me that the "God question" is really a Jesus question, and the Jesus question is really a "self question," and the two are inescapably joined: "Who do *you* say I am?"

To live a spiritual life, I need to follow the Spirit, and the Spirit's whole mission is to lead us into the way of Jesus, the way of incarnation. Why did it take me so long to discover this basic lesson of the gospel?

The Catholic Church has been struggling with the question of Jesus from the beginning. Especially in the first five centuries, members of the Church had a difficult time trying to give expression to their faith in Jesus. Today, twenty centuries later, the Church throughout the world still struggles with this Jesus question.

The solemnly defined doctrines of our faith in Jesus are few and abstract. These doctrines are simple and mysterious and wonderful. But, how do I live them? How does Jesus come alive in my heart? How do I come alive in Jesus and really desire to follow him? How do we really get involved with Jesus in this "spiritual life"?

It is one thing to affirm the truth of our faith: Jesus Christ is really, truly, fully God and really, truly, fully man. The human nature and divine nature are hypostatically united in the Word, Second Person of the Blessed Trinity. These two natures are each complete, yet remain distinct, while both are hypostatically united in the person of the Word.

My past inclination, and, I believe, the inclination of most Catholics, was to assent to this abstract formulation of the truth of the Incarnation.

I know and believe all the dogmas about Jesus. My act of faith is simple and unambiguous. Yet, it doesn't set me on fire! I cannot say I really know Jesus. I hardly know this person who is God, but who is also flesh and blood. I can't say I know much about his human experience as a little boy, as a teenager. I don't know how he felt about himself, especially if he got pimples or dropped a fly ball. Was he ashamed of his nose? How fast could he run? How far could he throw a ball? I don't know if he really liked girls. I don't know how he felt when he came home late or forgot to do the chores Joseph asked him to do.

There is so much about Jesus that I don't know. Indeed, I hardly know him at all. Then, it hit me—Jesus is *human*! I can discover Jesus in human experience, in *my* experience.

So, the question took a wondrous new turn. How will I ever learn about Jesus if I don't learn about my own human condition? How can I come to know (and follow) Jesus if I don't dare to become human myself (the way of incarnation)?

I was fascinated by the task before me. I began to feel something stirring inside me, a kind of longing, desire, even a sort of hunger. I really would like to get to know Jesus. I wanted to accept the question he gave me: "Who do you say I am?"

Let me share a couple of other experiences in my life about this time that helped me to rediscover Jesus.

I had been teaching moral theology for seven years (1958-1965). Then Vatican II insisted that moral theology should be renewed. This renewal meant returning to the Scriptures and rediscovering Jesus and our calling to follow him faithfully and lovingly for the life of the world.

This was a different focus for morality and spirituality. In a new way I had to take seriously the Jesus who asks: "Who do you say I am?"

This was exciting. It meant our moral and spiritual life must be rooted and centered in the person of Jesus, not a code of law. How could I teach morality, the following of Jesus, if I didn't

17

get to know him in a much more personal way?

What were the implications of Jesus' humanness and my own humanness? I had to learn a whole new approach to morality and spirituality with Jesus as the center. Thank God, I was not alone. Countless theologians and laypersons and religious all over the world were wrestling with the same question: "Who do you say I am?"

Another experience in my life about this time was the challenge of giving retreats and renewal workshops to communities of sisters. They were hungry for the Word of God, eager for the new life and ministry opened up to them by Vatican II.

They too heard anew the question of Jesus: "Who do you say I am?" In their prayer, community life and ministry they were searching to know Jesus. They desired a more personal and more scriptural understanding of the mystery of Jesus incarnate.

I was touched by them and their eagerness to know Jesus. In ministering to these sisters I was touched with grace through them. I heard Jesus loud and clear: "Who do you say I am?"

I found that people had been confused and misled by our preaching and teaching. So many people had come to mistrust their own experience, their own instincts and intuitions. They really did know Jesus, had a real "feel" for him in their daily lives, but were afraid to trust their hearts.

Many were confused by what was in their heads, especially their negative understanding of life and freedom, self-denial and mortification. These distorted understandings often meant rejecting the human condition.

These were people who struggled to lead good lives. They were so relieved, so overjoyed, to be encouraged to trust in their experience, to trust their hearts.

In ministering to the sisters I got to know many of them personally. This contact with women year after year became a powerful grace in my life, calling me to get in touch with myself, my humanness, as never before. I found Jesus in wondrous and beautiful and powerful ways through these women.

I believe the greatest grace in my life in the years

immediately following Vatican II was this burning question of Jesus. In a quiet but persistent way I took up the question. In prayer, in study, in teaching, in preaching, in counseling, in formation work, this intriguing question kept drawing me: "Who do you say I am?"

Gradually in lots of little ways, I found myself forced to look into my own experience. I found myself beginning to ask: What has Jesus to do with my experience? How can I find Jesus, come to know who Jesus is, by bringing faith to bear on my ordinary, daily experience?

I came to believe that personal growth and development, both as human and as Christian, was dynamic, cyclic and communitarian. I grow through a process of reflection—in the light of faith—on my experience. Books, classes, lectures, as well as professors, are all important resources, but I grow only from within, through this ongoing process of reflection on my human, Christian experience.

This change of focus and direction brought me new hope. More than ever I began to feel that life could make sense. I began to feel that I really could come to know who Jesus is, not by going on some far-off journey or climbing some intellectual tower, but by looking into my own experience in the light of faith and Scripture. I had discovered the hidden treasure in the field of my experience.

Moved by grace, I began digging. I even got excited. It was hard work, but I began to find tiny glimmers of who Jesus is. I slowly began to alter the way I prayed, the way I preached, the way I related to others.

It's hard to put into words. Saint Paul struggled with it too. His way of putting it was "to live is Christ Jesus," or "for me to live is Christ, to die is gain," or, "I live, now not I, but Christ lives in me."

Especially noticeable was the change in the way I taught morality and spirituality. I stopped bringing a bunch of books to every class for quoting "approved" authors. I began the daring project of putting into words the meaning of my own experience of living a morally good life; I tried to formulate my own understanding of morality and spirituality.

By reflecting on my own experience and struggles I tried to

discover who Jesus is and how his dying and rising was happening in my life. I tried to align my priorities with the gospel.

Another area in which the Jesus question kept pestering me was in counseling (both in spiritual direction and in the confessional). In these one-to-one situations, as I sought to focus on each person as a human person, and as I approached each with respect and reverence, I began to realize more clearly that Jesus was gracefully and powerfully active in each person, drawing each through his or her daily experience to new conversion. I was filled with wonder and awe at this mystery. Jesus somehow became more real to me as I saw him alive and active in others' lives.

As a spiritual director I aimed to assist people to consider their experiences in the light of faith and the gospel, in light of Jesus and the grace of the Spirit. In this relationship, we both discovered the face of Jesus. We both got a better sense of who Jesus is. We both felt drawn to follow Jesus more closely.

Finally, I began to discover who Jesus is in the sufferings I experienced. The period of the seventies was a time of deep pain in my life. I was between forty-five and fifty-five years old. I was going through the change of life and a lot of other changes, too.

As a teacher I was deeply concerned about the confusion and ambiguity in my field of moral/spiritual theology. There was so much disagreement among theologians, that, at times, I was ready to give up.

I also felt left out, even rejected by my own Franciscan province and the friars I lived with. I felt unappreciated and taken for granted. I knew in my head that this was not true, but I felt it, and, worse, did not realize what I was feeling or why I was angry.

I suffered also because of my anger and frustration with the official teachers of the Church—the pope and bishops. I felt especially frustrated with the Vatican Congregation of the Doctrine of the Faith. I felt they did not understand; they did not care; people were being greatly harmed. I myself was judged and rejected by bishops who didn't even know me. I felt disloyal for even questioning some points of official teaching.

I felt guilty. I felt hurt and angry.

It was a tough time for me. I really didn't think I would make it through this seemingly endless period. But, the Spirit kept touching me in gentle and graceful ways through some beautiful and caring people and some hopeful events.

I came not only to realize in a whole new way who Jesus is not only as one who suffered, but also as one who suffered freely, willingly and for us, for me! He accepted his human condition and he got hurt.

I began to understand how Jesus learned real obedience through what he suffered. In and through my sufferings, I began to know Jesus as gentle, poor and humble. I even began to think I was not hopeless. I felt tinglings of new life, new hope! The way of incarnation inevitably leads to the way of the cross. But, I discovered—finally—that it also leads to risen life!

CHAPTER THREE

To Be or Not to Be—
A Human Person

We are created and loved by God—loved precisely as human persons. As humans we are called to share divine life (grace). All the ways God comes to us, all the ways we are touched by God's grace, profoundly affect our existence, our human experience, our human be-ing. Grace always comes to us, affects us, as the humans we are.

We are not just human *beings*. We are human *persons*, capable of conscious thought and free choice. We are persons, aware of the world, things, people. We are capable of knowing and loving other persons, capable of relationships. As persons we are enmeshed in a complex web of relationships; we are rooted in society, communities, family.

God is calling us to become (come to *be*) more fully a human person, to develop our human and personal gifts and potential. God's love and grace calls us to ever fuller growth (conversion).

To become a human person means to grow as a balanced, harmonious whole. Intelligence, for example, is an important human capacity, but the person is much more than a brain. To be, or not to be human persons, is the question at the heart of our spiritual life.

The biggest challenge of following Jesus is not to keep the commandments, not to be a successful preacher, teacher, housewife or auto mechanic. The biggest challenge of following Jesus is to become a lover, a person who loves as Jesus loves, humanly and gracefully. (There's no other kind of genuine loving in this world!)

I find it amazing that every person I've ever met is engaged in the same kind of struggles, joy and pain, fears and anxieties as I am. These struggles may take different forms and shapes, but at the heart we are all engaged in the struggle to become human, to find meaning in our lives, to love and be loved, to fill the deep emptiness and longing of our hearts, to find our way home.

I Am a Human Person

My story of becoming holy, of following the Spirit, of leading a spiritual life, is a story of coming to know and appreciate myself as a human person.

It seems so strange to state the obvious: I am a human person. But, for so many years, it wasn't obvious to me at all. For many years, it didn't seem evident or important.

In my early years, I was raised to be obedient, to do what I was told. The most important thing was to please others, do what they asked. Who I was, was not important. It was not even considered. It was taken for granted.

This is pretty normal for children. The trouble with me was I didn't grow out of it. In my teens I attended high school seminary and found myself in a system where obedience was the order of the day. God help you if you got out of line. I became somewhat inwardly rebellious, but when the chips were down, I did what I was told by those in authority. It was important to me, to my self-worth (and to my "vocation"), to please others.

This was accentuated even more while in the novitiate. Now, being obedient would soon be sanctified by vow. Doing what others told me to do, following all the rules and laws, was to become holy and pleasing to God.

Every child, every teenager, deals with this problem in one way or another. Everyone must deal with authority (parent, teacher, pastor, police officers, employer, etc.). The rules and structure of society demand that we do what we are told, that we live by norms outside ourselves. At times this means conforming to what others want and even demand.

The challenge for all of us is to grow up! Rejecting or rebelling against authority is not growing up but rather remaining enslaved to the authority we fight against. The challenge of growing up is to stand on our own two feet, to perceive the values (the good) presented by authority (enfleshed in laws) and somehow make those values our own.

Gradually we grow in making our own decisions, taking responsibility for our own lives. We discover that obedience and freedom are not opposed. There is no virtuous obedience unless we freely choose to obey. Thus we become adults.

This is difficult because in many ways our behavior is conditioned by our parents and the way they led us to behave. We carry these patterns of behavior into our adult lives. Most of the time we're not even aware of them. We don't know how unfree we are. We don't realize how much of our lives is dictated by what others think or want. It's very difficult for anyone to become his or her own person.

I became a law-abiding citizen, a dependable and faithful worker, an obedient friar. I did not think of myself as a person; much less did I appreciate what being a person meant.

I was not aware of my *uniqueness*. I would have thought it vain or proud even to think I was uniquely gifted and graced, that I was really and deeply different from every other person. I was taught to feel best about myself when I was in step with others. I felt virtuous when I was a cog in a wheel. I felt accepted when I was obedient and law-abiding.

In school I found much of my self-worth in what I could *do*, especially on the ballfield and in the classroom. I felt good about myself when I hit a homerun or got the highest test score. This was especially true when the competition was fierce and I won!

All this began to change. I read psychology books that focused on the person and personal growth. New philosophical theories stressed the person, the existential, human experience. Scripture was being presented in new ways that stressed the concrete experience of real people with a living God; the primacy of love (rather than the Law) was emphasized. Moral theology began to focus on the moral person, the human and subjective aspects of behavior, personal freedom, interpersonal relations, history, culture, etc.

At first, I didn't know what to make of all this. My world (inner and outer) was cracking. My ideas about life—moral, religious, spiritual—were being challenged and found wanting. I felt lost, confused, helpless. I didn't know what to do! I didn't know where to go. I floundered, but thank God, I didn't run away. I kept reading, kept talking, kept going—somehow hoping there was light at the end of the tunnel.

In my prayer, studies, teaching, I found new meaning in the process of becoming human, in coming to know and accept myself as a person. I believed that I would find Jesus in the stuff of my ordinary, human, messy, mixed-up, confused, broken life.

In the mid-1950's I taught theology in summer school for more than one hundred Franciscan sisters. I was overwhelmed! I got to know some by name; some beginning friendships developed. I remember being drawn to these women. I was fascinated. I was afraid. I was self-conscious. I experienced a new glimmering of being human. I also remember distinctly a new sense of the presence of Jesus, though I didn't know what to make of that.

About this same time I became chaplain, teacher and spiritual director at St. Francis College in Fort Wayne, Indiana, a small college for women. Here I lived closely with the sisters, other faculty and also students. I don't know how effective I was in my teaching or ministry to them, but they taught me much! I was careful not to get *too* close (as I had been taught), and consequently was stiff and aloof most of the time. At the same time, these women won my heart and I have never been the same since!

I became aware of myself in new ways, and I became conscious of *them* (the women) in new ways too! I became aware of myself as a male as never before. My imagination at times ran wild. I became aware that I could have feelings of many kinds, especially feelings of tenderness and gentleness, as well as strong feelings of genital sexual desires.

In so many ways these women gave me such gifts of self-awareness. Without much conscious thought, I began to feel better about myself. I was no longer just brains and brawn.

I developed a respect for myself and others as persons.

In the early 1960's I conducted thirty-one-day renewal programs for groups of about thirty sisters. I lectured for three hours each day, held private consultations and celebrated Eucharist. I got to know each sister rather well. They shared much of themselves with me. The thirty-one days were draining for me but grace-filled.

I recall vividly that at the end of each program, the farewells were joyous and tearful, full of hugs and kisses. I had never hugged or kissed a woman, much less thirty of them. I remember feeling wonderful, full of life. Never was I so conscious of my self.

As I look back on these experiences now, I know them to have been powerful times of grace. Jesus was very close to me. His Spirit was very much at work in me. The fruits would not be evident for some time, but the fruits did come.

During all this I didn't really know what was happening and I would never have identified the movement as incarnational spirituality. I only knew that I clung to this new direction as a drowning person clung to a lifeline. Somehow, by the grace of God, I stayed afloat. It's no exaggeration to say that this movement toward a spiritual life rooted in the human has saved my life.

I Am a *Created* Human Person

In recent years I have begun to discover something of the depth and richness of being a creature. In seeking to know, appreciate and accept myself as a person, I found myself face to face with my creatureliness. It was revealing, even unsettling, but it was a whole new experience of Jesus.

It came home to me in a new way that Jesus became a creature. My call is to follow Jesus. As I follow Jesus in becoming human, so I follow him in becoming a creature.

It is true that I have been created (past), that I am a creature now (present). What I had failed to appreciate is that I need to *become* a creature (future). I need to recognize and be grateful for God's creative loving me now. I must respond to God's love by entering into my creatureliness, morally and spiritually living it, and so *becoming* creaturely.

If I don't enter into being dependent on God in all I am, I am rejecting who I am. If I don't accept being finite and limited, I try to be "god" and fall into the death of pride. Unless I enter into my vulnerability, I try to run away from pain and suffering. Thus, I miss the heart of life and the thrill of growth. If I set myself apart from other creatures, I condemn myself to a life of loneliness and incompleteness.

The following insights helped me appreciate my creatureliness better and so opened me to new ways of discovering Jesus in my daily experiences.

Dependent

As a creature I am dependent on God. God loves me into being. God is the source of all that I am, the source of my *be*-ing, the source of all that I can *come to be*. God is the source of my being bodily, spiritual, sensual, emotional, sexual, intellectual, volitional, imaginative, remembering.

I am utterly dependent on God in relationships and in community. I am completely dependent on God in all the expressions of my self: all my words, thoughts, deeds; all my judging and choosing and deciding; all my valuing and prioritizing; all my deepest hopes, longings, desires, etc. Note that God is not the cause of my sinful actions. But if God did not sustain me in being, I could not express myself at all.

God is source of my *all*! No wonder Saint Francis would cry out over and over, "My God, my All!" No wonder Jesuits take as their motto: "All to the Greater Glory of God."

I sense myself as free. I pride myself in being independent. I have felt I didn't need anyone else. I could stand on my own feet, make my own way. For so many years I've made so many decisions and expressed myself in all kinds of behavior, and I've had little or no sense of being dependent on God or other people. I could get the job done. I could handle things and people. I was in control. How very mistaken I was.

Eventually I was brought face to face with my weakness. In

time my world began to fall apart, when I began to see—and admit—my powerlessness, my helplessness. I discovered that I needed God. In this, I found Jesus in a new way.

To some extent I stopped running away from my helplessness. I found that if I could accept and embrace my limitations, I could experience what Jesus did. His helplessness I experienced in my own. He could relive his in mine. I found that Jesus did not remove my helplessness, but he gave me the grace to accept it. He gave me the strength to go on with my life, limited as I am.

After finding Jesus in my helplessness, I didn't have to do extraordinary deeds to become holy. The call to holiness is in my "here and now" experiences. Jesus is present; the grace is offered. Every moment is a moment of salvation.

I marveled to find that in admitting my own dependency on God, I could admit I was creature. I belonged to God. I was "of God"; I was made "for God." I discovered something precious about my self. I am valuable, even prior to my "works." I am sacred.

Now I began to see everything differently. I felt differently about others, myself and all creatures. For example, it hit me that all evil is desecration of a creature of God.

The practical question arose: How can I find new ways of coming to be (becoming) dependent on God. How can I live this dependency and not just think about it? How can I experience it in my daily life? Somehow I felt my developing sense of dependency was the key to new growth.

It's a paradox! In my efforts to accept my dependence on God, I was growing up. In entering into this experience of belonging to God, I came to greater freedom and independence. I had less need to be in control. By accepting my limitations, I could live more fully. In accepting my imperfections I could be truer to myself. Thus, the way opened up to new possibilities for change, for growing up in Christ.

For example, in my daily walk I am continually lost in amazement and gratitude. I feel being able to walk, breathe, see, feel, smell, think, remember as experiences of my dependency on God. Without God I could do none of these. This sense of dependency does not lead me to feel discouraged

29

that I'm not bigger or more independent; rather I feel a sense of joy and peace, of well-being and gratitude. It feels good to depend on God! I am held in the palm of God's hands.

I also experience my dependency when I find pennies and other coins while walking. As I walk I almost always find coins. It seems funny, but it has become a rather moving experience. Each of these pennies has become a "sacrament" of Jesus present, a sign that *all* is gift. I sometimes become preoccupied looking for coins. Sometimes I find a quarter, and then I am disappointed when I find "only" a penny. I discover how greedy I am.

I learn that even the tiniest gift is still gift and sign of God's love. I find a penny, and Jesus reminds me again: "I am still with you"! I walk a long time and find nothing, and Jesus challenges me to look for the giver more than the gifts. I find a penny and am again surprised: Jesus asks me if I feel abandoned. And so it goes.

This new sense of being totally dependent on God in all I am brings with it a new sense of being "little." I'm beginning to understand Jesus: "Unless you become as little children...." I was struck, almost as though I had never thought of it before, I am finite. I am limited! I am so very little!

Finite, Limited

When seen in light of being human, my limitations seem evident. Yet, I find it hard to admit my imperfections, not to mention my weakness and failings and sinfulness. A spirituality built on nonacceptance of being a creature is not healthy.

A few years ago, as I began a talk to a small group of Franciscans of a different province, I noticed a statue of Saint John the Baptist. I said to those present: "I come to you from the Province of Saint John the Baptist, and like the Baptist, I must state emphatically, 'I am not the messiah! I am not the Christ!' I am just a little friar, here to serve you." As I said this I remember shivering; I was moved almost to tears. It hit me like a flash of lightning. I suddenly thought: It's true! I am not

God! I cannot save the world! Why do I act as if I am, and could? It was a strange experience of God's grace.

Some of the sisters I know, sisters who are dear to me, called me—in jest, I trust—"Jahweh Junior." At first I thought that was a compliment. It finally dawned on me that I often tried to be God. I found it difficult to admit that I do not have unlimited power or energy, that I could not say yes to every request. I do not have unlimited intelligence or freedom, or *anything*.

It was hard for me to accept myself as a creature, as limited. Strangely, however, the more I thought about this, and prayed about it, I could almost feel myself relaxing. It was like letting out a deep breath. I felt lighter, more at peace, more free. I began to say to myself: "It's OK to be human! It's OK to be limited."

I began to experience the care and tenderness and mercy of Jesus much more when I dared admit I was finite, limited. I could stop acting as though I was everyone's savior (that's a heavy burden!). I could open myself to Jesus and admit my littleness. In my need I could ask him to be strength and savior to me.

There is such pride involved in my attempts to "play God," to act as though I had answers to everyone's difficulties, to insist that my ideas were the right ones, that my ways of doing things were better.

Jesus was more powerfully present and active in me and in others when I left some room for him, when I found my place in preparing his way instead of trying to take his place.

I discovered humility. The more I gave attention to the meaning and implications of being limited, the more I began to discover true humility. Pride (which is indeed the "original sin") is evident when I try to play God. To be humble is to be and live in the truth. The truth is, I am human, imperfect, weak, a sinner.

This truth is liberating. As I admitted my weakness and imperfection, I became more free, more human. The more I could accept my own weakness, the better I could minister to others. In a word, the more I accepted being little and finite, the more Jesus could make himself known to me. Paul's words are to the point: "I will rather boast most gladly of my weaknesses, in order that the power of Christ may dwell with me" (2 Corinthians 12:9).

Perhaps most importantly, as I came to accept my limitations, I could be gentle and compassionate with others. I was less demanding of myself and them. The more I allowed myself to be human, I could accept others as human, as not perfect. In this I came to know Jesus, gentle and humble of heart.

I always felt attracted to Jesus' words, "Learn of me, for I am gentle and humble of heart," but found them hard to practice. Now, I began to see how Jesus related to little children, to the poor, to ordinary persons. I began to get a "feel" for Jesus and his mercy for sinners. In facing my own limitations, weakness, brokenness, I began to feel more gentle, more tender with others in their brokenness. To become humble means entering into the truth of my finite human condition and accepting it as the place where I find God.

In contrast, I began to realize, with a kind of fear, how proud, arrogant and conceited I really am! I can be so demanding, hard, lacking in understanding and patience.

Sometimes I feel "humble" when I deny my gifts and talents. When I run myself down, claim I'm a sinner, bad mouth myself, while unconsciously trying to control others, I am proud, not humble.

At times I have become very angry at another person—loud and abusive, verbally violent and threatening, utterly disrespectful of the other person. Usually this happened with someone I loved (someone who would not hurt me back) when the other person did not understand me or would not accept my ideas or would not do what I thought best.

When this happened, I felt terrible, not so much because I had hurt another, but because I had failed so miserably. (I assumed I was supposed to be perfect.) I found it almost impossible to forgive myself. I was imprisoned in my pride, in my refusal to accept my brokenness.

Vulnerable

Another aspect of being a creature is being vulnerable. Until
recently I had not paid attention to this. I've been healthy,
strong, energetic all my life. I found it difficult to think of
myself as frail, weak, susceptible to pain, hurt, sickness,
suffering, disease, even death.

I will deal with this much more completely in Chapter
Seven.

One With All Creatures

As I slowly came to accept being a creature, I found my
relatedness to all other creatures demanding attention. Saint
Francis developed a special kinship toward animals. He felt a
bond with every creature, so much so that in deep reverence he
called them "brother" or "sister." For example, he spoke of
"brother sun" and "sister moon."

Saint Francis has much to teach me about being a creature
of God. Francis reminds me that if I don't reverence the earth
and every creature, I sell myself short. I don't know who I am.

I don't really feel much kinship with other creatures. I walk
the earth as though it's not there. I breathe the air and drink the
water with hardly a thought. I am rather oblivious of my union
with birds and fish. I just assume they will always be there. I
take the sun for granted...until the lights go out! I pay little
attention to sister water...until the well runs dry.

During the oil embargo of 1973, I remember the lines at the
filling stations and my anger that the price was increasing.
Schools were closed that winter because they had no heating
oil.

Gradually it began to dawn on me. The resources of the
earth are limited, finite. The supply of oil or water or anything
is not endless. If I squander these created resources, they're
gone. Those who come after me will be without. I may use
these resources, but with reverence and respect and
responsibility to the future.

The oil embargo opened my eyes to the broader picture, to

the way I take other creatures for granted. It opened my eyes to the fact that I abuse water, air, ground. I am wasteful and destructive of trees, wood, paper and metals. I waste food, plants, flowers, books.

I share in the evil of polluting the air and water. I am involved in the use of insecticides and pesticides. I can't hold myself aloof of the destruction of our rain forests, wetlands, ozone layer. It's amazing that in this incredible technological age, we can't even find ways to deal with our garbage without polluting the environment.

While it is right and good to make use of creatures for the service of persons and human society, we do not have any right to rape the earth, to plunder creation, to pollute the world for immediate and inordinate amassing of wealth.

I am a creature. I may be a human person, with intelligence and freedom, but I am still a creature. I am inherently bonded, as creature, with every other creature (human, animal, plant, inanimate). In a mysterious way we are one. I need to hear the "sounds of silence"; I need to hear the rivers sing; I need to bleed when a tree is cut; I need to hear the cry of the wolf, the song of the birds. I need to attend to the whisper of the wind and the roar of the ocean. I need to come to be "in tune" with my brothers and sisters of the universe.

When I was a youngster on the farm, I loved to go barefoot and feel the earth between my toes. I still remember planting sweet potato plants in the warm moist earth in the spring, watering and hoeing them through the summer and digging them with bare hands in the fall. I felt close to mother earth; I was amazed at the fruitfulness of the earth. In moments of joy I would tiptoe so as to walk gently on mother earth.

I learned these and other lessons as a youngster. I forgot them when I grew up. I became careless, wasteful, even abusive and destructive. In the process I became somewhat inhuman.

A few years ago I came across words attributed to Seattle, Chief of the Suquamish. In response to a proposed treaty to buy Indian land, he is supposed to have said:

How can you buy or sell the sky, the warmth of the land? The idea is strange to us. If we do not own the freshness of the air and the sparkle of the water, how can you buy them? Every part of this earth is sacred to my people. Every shining pine needle, every sandy shore, every mist in the dark woods, every clearing and humming insect is holy in the memory and experience of my people. The sap which courses through the trees carries the memories of the red man.

These words had a deep influence on me, and I began to pray about my relation to other creatures, to every other creature. So many people in spiritual direction, or in directed retreats, told me how they found God in nature, how they discovered Jesus in creation. I didn't realize what I had been missing.

Paul's words in the Letter to the Romans are very pertinent:

For creation awaits with eager expectation the revelation of the children of God;...in hope that creation itself would be set free from slavery to corruption and share in the glorious freedom of the children of God. We know that all creation is groaning in labor pains even until now; and not only that, but we ourselves, who have the firstfruits of the Spirit, we also groan within ourselves as we wait for adoption, the redemption of our bodies. (Romans 8:19, 21-23)

I am a creature. What mystery! This says so much of who I am; it says so much about who God is to me; it says so much of who I am with every other creature.

I am a creature, an unfolding, unfinished mystery. I am not yet all that I can come to be. I am more and more coming to be a creature.

I am more and more becoming dependent on God and accepting my limitations. I am opening myself to my vulnerability, my imperfections. In accepting them, I am in a better position to grow.

I am more and more seeking to enter into the deep, wondrous potential of being created in God's image: a human person, aware, free, responsible, loving.

I am a creature. Jesus, the Word-made-flesh, is a creature. I am creature in him. He is creature in me. In entering more and more into creatureliness he embraces me; I discover him; he lives in me.

CHAPTER FOUR

Holiness Is Wholeness

Some years ago the statement "holiness is wholeness" was popular. These words clearly indicate that we ought not insert barriers between the holy and the human, the sacred and the profane. The dynamics of human growth and integration are also the dynamics of becoming holy persons, spiritual persons.

The way of Jesus, the way of incarnation, is our human way. The power and influence of God's grace moves us to become holy and more fully human at one and the same time and in one and the same process. Life as a growing human person, and life as a growing Christian, is one life. "Holiness is wholeness."

In the next chapter we will reflect on specific aspects of being human and experiencing Jesus in our daily lives. There we'll look at our struggle to know, appreciate, accept and live out our bodiliness, our senses, our feelings, our sexuality. In all this we are living out our spiritual lives.

In this chapter I will consider three aspects of my very *self*, three aspects of my human and personal wholeness: I am one person; I am a person of mystery and depth; I am a developing person.

This chapter is more abstract. I want to share the fruits of my efforts to reflect on my experience and understand myself more deeply. All of this helped me understand who I am. It shed light on my spiritual life. I hope my reflections might help you.

What You See Is What You Get—Me!

As a created human person, as a graced human person, I am one. All of me is *me*! It seems rather self-evident to say that. Yet, in many ways I experience the opposite. I experience not being one; I experience brokenness, fragmentation.

The experience of brokenness, of being torn apart, of lacking inner (and outer) peace, touched me deeply. I remember being pulled in different directions in prayer. At times I hated and loved my friends at the same time. I was torn by contradictory feelings when my dad died: glad and sad, burdened and free.

God doesn't create chaos. The wondrous fact is that, in spite of my brokenness, in a deep way I am *one*. My brokenness tends to hide this inner oneness. I need to be in touch with this deep oneness because it is at one and the same time my present source of strength and my future hope.

At the very heart of this "crisis of oneness" is the Greco-Roman conception that the human being is composed of body and soul. This conception has been commonly accepted in the Western world for more than twenty centuries. It is embedded in our language, our culture, our theology and our spirituality.

This body-soul conception does have some value, but it also has definite limits and inadequacies. It leaves much unsaid about being human.

The body-soul model focuses on human nature, rather than the human person. This focus has created problems for me. In time I became aware that this view is associated with some unacceptable, even harmful, implications for spirituality.

Harmful implications. The body is considered material, while the soul is spiritual. Some have held that all matter is evil, and so the body too is evil. Others have held that the body is not evil, but is much less worthy than the soul, and is therefore unimportant and secondary to the soul.

The soul is spiritual and far nobler than the body. Our goal in life is to "save our souls." The body is just not important. So, the spiritual becomes identified with the soul, and spirituality is more and more removed from our daily lives and experience. I remember the stress put on spiritual exercises, such as praying the rosary, going to Mass. These helped our spiritual life. Playing ball, going to a movie—these didn't count for heaven.

Feelings don't count. If the body is second-rate, then, since feelings belong to the body (not the soul), they are not important. So, I came to downgrade my feelings, even reject them. This leads to devastating consequences in understanding myself. I found it practically impossible to appreciate my oneness as a human person.

No wonder I had great difficulty in coming to grips with my feelings. I denied my feelings, acted as though I didn't have them or sought to repress them. This made it difficult for me to relate to others and communicate on any sort of personal level. It was hard for me to form deep and lasting relationships.

Sex misunderstood. I learned that sexuality is limited to the genital organs and so to the body. It was implied that the soul was in no way sexual. If the body is second-rate, so is sexuality. I also learned the predominant way of dealing with my sexuality was to deny it or ignore it.

This led me to misunderstand my sexuality, to misunderstand myself. Yet, since sexuality is such a pervasive aspect of myself, I felt divided.

Mistrust of senses. I also learned to mistrust my senses. God gave us these five incredible openings to the outer world as ways to be in touch with others and with the rest of creation. God gave us the capacity to see, hear, feel, taste and smell. I did not learn that I needed to use these senses well and to give thanks to God for them. I learned to be fearful of them. The senses could lead me astray—looking at the wrong things, impure feelings and touches, etc. Sensuality came to have an evil meaning.

These consequences of the unhealthy split between body-soul in the area of the senses, feelings and sexuality most obviously involve the body. Other harmful consequences of this split involve the soul more directly.

Intellectualizing life. One of the powers of human persons is rationality. Aristotle defined the human being as a "rational animal." He emphasized rationality as that which distinguishes us from animals. In time the importance of the power of reason, noble and wonderful as it is, was exaggerated. Eventually for many "being human" meant "being reasonable." When this was accompanied by downplaying feelings, reason was blown out of proportion. I experienced this. I was intellectually gifted; I often denied my feelings. I did well in school, but not in daily life.

Conscience is one of the areas in which this exaltation of reason became evident. Making decisions about my actions, about what was right and wrong, was complicated. Decisionmaking was like an intellectual game. Finding ways to avoid obeying laws was a challenge. This did not help me mature in moral responsibility.

Another consequence of this exaggeration of rationality was that I was able to talk about God, prayer, the spiritual life. Talking became equivalent to doing it, living it. Unwittingly I accepted the saying attributed to Plato: "Knowledge is virtue." Yet, the terrible fact is that knowledge, as such, never made anyone holy!

Voluntarism. A similar harm to my spiritual life resulted when I exaggerated the importance of my will. "Voluntarism" says that as a human being I have a free will, and if I want to overcome some temptation, some weakness (such as alcoholism or drug addiction), all I have to do is "make up my mind," decide to do it and then *do it.* If I fail, it simply means that I did not really want to do it; I didn't use my free will; I wasn't determined enough. Put simply, this extreme form of voluntarism holds that "I can do anything I want; just use my willpower, and do it."

This overlooks the fact that the human person is one. I cannot do anything I want just by willing it. I am subject to all kinds of influences. I am free to a certain extent, but in many ways I am not free. My freedom is limited, situated, conditioned. Carrying out my free choices is complicated and involves many factors. My free will is limited by my background, my education, my past growth and development, my feelings, my weaknesses and the like. All this must be taken into consideration before I can "make up my mind" and do it!

The nonhistorical approach. Another consequence of overemphasizing the importance of the soul to the detriment of the body is the nonhistorical approach to life and spirituality.

My family roots, my cultural inheritance, the people in my past life—none of the dimensions of history and culture are important. It's a strange, erroneous and tragic application of Paul's preaching that, "It is the spirit that counts; the flesh is worthless."

This has grave consequences for my understanding of who I am, of the meaning of my life and how God is at work in my daily life. Religion and life, nature and grace, this life and the next, prayer and daily activity, the sacred and the secular—everything seemed to be moving in different directions. I felt divided—inwardly and outwardly.

I am one. I have come to see the importance of my *oneness* as a human person. I am bodily (rooted in space and time, of the earth) and I am spiritual (ensouled, able to transcend space and time). As one person I have many powers, abilities, capacities. It is I who think, will, feel, sense, remember, imagine. I am one. I function as one. I experience as one. I love and relate as one. Underneath all my brokenness and dividedness I am one person.

I live my spiritual life as one. In a way, then, the goal of conversion, of spiritual growth, is integration, "getting it all together," becoming more and more one—in my self, in my relationships and in all of life. To be at one with God is my ultimate goal.

There's More to Me Than Meets the Eye!

I am mystery! There is so much more to each person than meets the eye. God is infinitely mysterious, and we are created in the image and likeness of Mystery. We are more than a social security number, so much more than what we do.

There is depth to the human person. As Scripture says, "man sees the appearance but the LORD looks into the heart" (1 Samuel 16:7). A new realization of this wondrous and mysterious depth of the human person is one of the most significant and far-reaching developments in morality and spirituality. It is a new insight, yet it's always been with us. It's new in that it was unnoticed for a long time. But it has been rediscovered in the past half-century.

This new awareness has profoundly influenced my understanding of morality of the heart, basic freedom and life orientation. This, in turn, deepens my appreciation of the moral and spiritual significance of my acts. Consequently, my understanding of freedom and responsibility, grace and sin, has changed.

It is natural for me to look into the mystery of "self" and be lost in wonder. I instinctively feel there is more to me than meets the eye. I am, in my saner moments, convinced that I am more than a "do-er." In fact, I feel let down when someone seems to appreciate me only for what I do.

This sense of the depth and mystery of the human person is most clearly and forcefully experienced when I come to love another. The one I begin to love becomes attractive, more and more mysterious. The beloved "takes my breath away," illumines my world, changes my outlook. Love leads me into an experience of reality far beyond my intellectual capacity. I've come to realize that I discover and experience God when I face the mystery of another person.

Then it dawns on me: This is not surprising! The Scriptures clearly indicate the profound depth of the human person. This is implicit in the call to covenant. It is inevitable when I ponder the mystery of being called to a relationship of love, knowledge and union with the Triune God: "Abide in me and I in you."

When I lose touch with this sense of inner mystery, I put more and more emphasis on outward actions. Spirituality becomes superficial, identified with "spiritual exercises." Morality becomes predominantly a matter of outward observance, and personal initiative, personal responsibility are not valued. It becomes easy to judge myself and others rashly, misunderstanding and misinterpreting actions.

In the past, I went to Mass, I fasted and abstained, I said my prayers, but so often I was not concerned about the inner meaning of what I did. I observed the laws outwardly; my heart may have been "on vacation."

Jesus, using the words of Isaiah, says to the people of his time: "This people honors me with their lips, but their hearts are far from me" (Matthew 15:8). Jesus refers to the behavior of the scribes and Pharisees, yet challenges his followers: "I tell you, unless your righteousness surpasses that of the scribes and Pharisees, you will not enter into the kingdom of heaven" (Matthew 5:20). Jesus refers to the inner mystery of the human person in the greatest commandment: "You shall love the Lord, your God, with all your heart, with all your soul, and with all your mind.... You shall love your neighbor as yourself" (Matthew 22:37, 39).

The more I pondered the mystery of the human heart, the more elusive it became. The more I sensed I was "in touch" with my heart, the less I could put it into words. The more I came to know my "self," the more I felt I needed still to learn. When I tried to "know my heart" directly, I was blinded.

Finally, it came to me: No one but God can "see into the human heart"; I can only see as in a glass, darkly. I have a "sense," and intuition of who I am, of my "self," but it is vague, undefined, shrouded in mystery. Gradually I came to believe that I come to know my "self," my heart indirectly, from the outside in, as it were.

When I look at one act of mine (for example, a single, isolated act of forgiveness), I really don't know what to make of it morally and spiritually. I can guess; I can presume, but I really don't know. If I find a *consistent pattern* of behavior, if I find that I am forgiving not only when it's easy but also when it's hard, then, in light of that consistent pattern, the single act takes on meaning. It is the expression of an inner value.

If I am patient not only when others see me but even when I'm alone, if I am patient consistently no matter what, then I know I value patience. There is no other reason for my consistent behavior.

So, patterns of consistent behavior reveal my values. When I discover a value I am committed to, I have seen a facet of who I am. I have come to know that I am a patient person. As I do this in other matters, I find out what *kind* of person I am. I am discovering facets of my "self," of my core, of my heart.

I am creating my heart, the "person" I am, in the consistent activation of my values through my daily choices and concrete behavior. All my choices, all my actions, are expressions of me. There is an incredible depth and meaning to all my ordinary humdrum activity. Washing the dishes, fixing a flat, drinking a martini are significant and meaningful actions. They are mine; they reveal me; they shape the mystery of me.

No longer can my life be boring. No longer can my daily activities be empty or dead. It's life-giving to give a tiny ordinary gift to my brother on his birthday. The gift is an outward sign of the inward reality. The gift is a sign of the love in my heart. My heart gives ultimate meaning to all my daily acts.

The goal, then, of my moral/spiritual life is to live and choose and act from the heart. The goal of all my striving is not only to do the good, but do it from the heart. My consuming desire is to live wholeheartedly. As the beer ad says: Live with gusto. You only go around once. In my life with God, I want to live with gusto, with enthusiasm, with heart.

I visualize three levels of myself as person. These are distinct aspects of the one person, mutually interrelated and functionally interdepent.

Outer level (acts, behavior, patterns). This outer level has to do with my actions, my behavior. It would, I think, also include the activities of my senses, feelings, intellect and will. It involves the more obviously perceptible aspect of my life.

Whenever I express myself, it shows up in my behavior. My actions are the more superficial level. Actions are important, yet even more important are the inner values that prompt my choices and give meaning to my actions.

In the past I gave excessive attention and importance to my actions. What I did was very important. Spirituality means putting my faith into action. The grace God gives me must bear fruit in good works.

But, in emphasizing outward deeds, I can fail to give due attention to my inner values. My outward actions have no meaning except in terms of inward values from which they spring. When I stress actions too much, I can become superficial.

I believe this superficiality, this undue focus on outward acts, flows especially from an excessive preoccupation with observance of laws. This overemphasis on observance of law, together with the failure to relate laws to the inner values that give them meaning, leads to legalism.

Legalism tends to jeopardize my commitment to gospel values of love, justice and so on. Legalism inclines me to a superficial approach to the moral and spiritual life. Indirectly this also inclines me to separate religion and life.

For example, I now see that a person is not to be praised or blamed simply because of what is done. I cannot presume a person is guilty simply because he or she did something evil. Nor is it enough just to do the right thing.

The goal of my moral life is to do good from the heart, to choose freely and wholeheartedly to follow the promptings of the Holy Spirit. God seeks my heart, not just lip-service. It is when I look to my depths, and seek to live from my depths, that I realize that "holiness is wholeness."

It is indeed important to take Jesus seriously: "Not everyone who says to me, 'Lord, Lord,' will enter the kingdom of heaven, but only the one who does the will of my Father in heaven" (Matthew 7:21). What is in the human heart must show up in outward deed. But, the ever present danger is to do the deed without our heart being in it. The risk is to live on the surface.

The important questions for my spiritual and moral life are: What is the *meaning* of my life? What is the meaning of what I do? Thus, I come to another question, a still more important question: *Why* do I do what I do?

Two concrete and specific questions in my life gave flesh and blood to this question of the meaning of my outward actions: the question of sexuality and the question of mortal sin.

Neither, I felt, could be treated adequately simply by looking at behavior. Genital-sexual actions, as such, could not reveal the goodness of purity or the evilness of impurity. The meaning of purity cannot be found in simply avoiding certain acts.

Likewise, guilt cannot be presumed simply because the person does evil deeds. How and when, and under what conditions, does a person become guilty of the evil deed he or she does? That is a question of actions, but it is much more than that.

I found the same questions arising with regard to prayer, friendship and intimacy, love of neighbor, commitment, fidelity, and so on. I had been taught to look at morality and spirituality primarily in terms of behavior. I sensed there has to be more to it!

I asked why. Why this law, or that? Why were we commanded to do certain things, forbidden to do others?

At first I pursued the "why" outwardly, that is, because of authorities. I did certain things, I avoided certain things, because I was told to do so. But I quickly discovered that this is not a real answer. The "why" did not go away; it was just pushed back. Why do those in authority give me these commands, these prohibitions?

Inner level (values, priorities). I moved to a deeper level and looked more deeply within my self. I discovered the "inner level" of moral habit, the inner level of values (which is also called the level of virtues and vices). This inner aspect of me involves my value system.

This value *system* is made up of the group of values that have become mine, that I know and appreciate and have become committed to over the course of many years. These values are the "good things" that are important to me, the deep convictions and principles I have come to live by (for example, freedom, justice, etc.).

These values shape me in a deep way. They make me the kind of person I am (friendly, understanding, compassionate, etc.). They guide my choices, they explain and give meaning to my behavior. These values reveal why I do what I do and why

I do the good I do consistently.

The second aspect of my value system is that it is not just a random list of values, not just a bunch of isolated virtues.

As I was growing up, becoming mature, I was not only committing myself to pursuing certain values, I was also developing my priorities. I was organizing my values into a consistent kind of system, a hierarchy.

When I make choices freely, choices that are my own, I do so because that is important (valuable) to me. I act because I am drawn to the good (value) involved.

Invariably, there is more than one value involved in a situation. No matter what choice I make, I cannot realize all the values. I have to make hard choices. I have to prefer one value to another. My choice will reveal not only my values, but also my priority of values, my preferences.

For example, it took a long time for me to come to appreciate and value friendship. When my relationships with a few persons did develop into friendships, they were important to me, but I always gave priority to other values, such as ministry or community. My friends took a back seat!

Whenever I do evil, it is because I prefer a lesser value to a greater value. That is moral disorder, an inversion of values. That is why my choice and act is evil. Love of neighbor is the supreme value, but the expression of love must be rightly ordered. This can be difficult, for I am also inclined to act selfishly.

I appreciated this mystery, this depth, this inner level of the human person and realized that here is the focus of conversion (reorganizing my priorities). Here is the focus of religious education. Knowledge is important, but it's never enough. Value formation is critical for living a good life.

Educating the whole person means value formation, value education. Only then can I hope that education will mean the spiritual growth of the whole person, a growth that bears fruit in good and holy living.

Information about values is not enough. Intellectual knowledge of values is important, but not adequate. I can know about purity, but not become pure. I will only live the value, make it my own, when it somehow becomes important to me, when I am so attracted to it that I'm willing to struggle to achieve it—and practice it consistently.

This inner level of values can be complicated, confusing and messy. For example, I tend to disagree with others in three ways. First, I often disagree with others about the expression of values. Is refusal to allow homosexuals into the military an act of discrimination? Is this act a violation of the virtue of justice?

Second, I disagree with others about the meaning of values. Justice, for example, means different things to different people!

Third, I disagree even more on how to prioritize values. Each one of us has a different sense of how to organize our values, how to order them in harmony with the gospel. What are the right priorities for a Christian?

I find I can discuss these matters endlessly in the abstract realm. In practice I am dealing with unique persons, with unique backgrounds, in unique situations. So, it is almost impossible to formulate laws that are valid, except quite general ones. Also, it is almost impossible to judge another person's guilt based on behavior.

Inmost level (my center, heart, self). Gradually, I saw that there is a depth to me, and to every person, that goes even beyond the inner level of values. I glimpsed my heart.

I saw that the gospel calls us to a moral and spiritual life that is from the heart. This was an astonishing discovery for me. I can say simply that it changed me, my outlook on life, my understanding of morality and spirituality. It brought me face to face with incarnational spirituality. For, in my heart, I caught a glimpse of "me"; in my heart I caught a glimpse of God.

When I first heard of morality of the heart from Father Bernard Häring, I was fascinated. It just seemed to be so on target. I had always felt uncomfortable with the emphasis and focus on outward behavior.

I remember feeling so puzzled about people who were supposedly "living in sin," people who were in "bad marriages." Yet I knew these people. I knew that in many basic ways they were such good persons.

There were many aspects of morality that didn't make sense. Looking into the depth of the person did not solve all the questions, but it opened up many hopeful doors.

As a teacher of morality, a preacher and a spiritual director, I was involved in many ways with the question of commitment: to God (question of grace and sin), perpetual commitment of baptism (question of living faith), commitment in marriage, religious life, priesthood. When seen in terms of the heart, of one's deepest self, these questions took on new meaning.

The person is ever mysterious and incomprehensible, even to oneself. I have the capacity to dispose of my whole self (basic freedom) in my practical choice to marry this person, profess these vows. When I do so, I express myself in this particular way to this person and to God. The expression of myself in the act of marriage or religious profession is a culmination of my whole life up to this point. It is a setting of my life-course for the future. It deeply involves me, you, God. It is indeed incarnational. It is a wondrous moment of deep personal self-expression. It is a moment of faith, hope, love. It is about as close to a fully moral and spiritual act as I can imagine.

As is evident, it is not perfect. My level of maturity is not static nor complete. If my deep, personal commitment (from the heart) is to bear fruit and endure, I must not only be able to make my commitment knowingly and freely here and now; I must freely keep it alive in my heart by the ongoing struggle to grow in fidelity.

In conclusion, let me take prayer as an example of both the distinctness and interrelatedness of these three levels of the human person.

The activity of praying is very important in our lives. A veritable mountain of books, tapes and articles deal with the importance of praying, different methods and techniques of praying, different effects of fidelity and regularity in praying.

Even more important than the activity of praying is the value of prayer, the inner meaning of prayerful activity. The fathers and doctors of the Church, the popes, the masters of the spiritual life all insist on the importance of praying. Why should I pray?

How does praying influence my sense of God, my relationship with God? How does it shape the kind of person I am, my outlook on life, the meaning of my daily life? How does prayer help me grow as a Christian? How does this activity help me love and serve my neighbor?

It seems to me that it's only when I wrestle with these questions and become aware of the deep meaning of praying, that I will see why it is important and valuable in my life with God and with other people. I will see that praying has meaning. It helps me live my life more fruitfully and grow in my life with God.

Finally, prayer becomes important to me because it helps me become a prayerful person. This activity is valuable to me because it gives shape to the way I want to live. It gives flesh and blood to the way I want to be and relate to God and other people.

This activity becomes important because it helps me incarnate my basic life orientation, my faith-commitment to God. It makes sense in terms of my heartfelt desire to live for God and neighbor.

'I Ain't Done Yet'

I remember well the many changes that took place after Vatican II. We weren't used to changes in the Church and many Catholics resisted these changes. Some would not attend Mass in English; others would have nothing to do with the Sign of Peace; others would never receive Communion from a layperson; others would not even consider going to confession face to face.

Dramatic and far-reaching changes were occurring in the world, in our country, in technology, in the media, in health care, in transportation. Yet, to so many, any change in the Catholic Church was betrayal, even if it did come from the pope and bishops!

God only knows the agony, the pain, the suffering all this brought about in people's lives and within families. I grew up with a strong sense that the Church is very stable, practically immutable; the Church would never change. Official teaching, especially in morality, practically never changed. Now, devotions, sacramental practices, laws were changing. Often these changes came without adequate education and preparation.

Change is a fact of life. In some ways I welcome change. I long for spring after winter. I look forward to a new job. I like to watch children grow into adulthood. In other ways, I face change reluctantly, or not at all. I don't want to go to school. I don't want to undergo surgery. I don't want to move.

Change we must. It's the human way. It's a fact of life for human families and societies. Change is inherent in every creature. It's change or die! As persons, we have the capacity to be aware of change, to guide and promote, to accept or reject change. We have the potential to become better through change or to become worse.

Change touches every facet of our being: physical, biological, physiological, emotional, affective, volitional, intellectual, relational, political, spiritual, moral, etc. I remember once seeing a sign: "Be gentle with me; I'm not done yet!"

The ancient Christians had a pointed way of saying it: In this life we are "on the way" (*in via*); only in the next life will we finally arrive "at home" (*in patria*).

Seen in the context of incarnational spirituality, all this changing is a matter of conversion, changing for the better. It affects me as a unique individual, as involved in interpersonal relations, as living in the midst of family, society, Church, world. This call to conversion is a movement that is always both human and divine, involving freedom and grace. Growing in the expression of human love means growth in holiness.

Conversion is a struggle to accept reality as it is (dying to my inordinate tendency to control and manipulate) so as to enter into reality as it can become (new creature, new life). It is a matter of letting go of all the facets of "being child" so as to enter into the ways of being adult.

Change, conversion, is a process of integration. As a child, a teenager, I'm pulled in many different directions, attracted to many "goods," and I want them all. I don't really know what I do want. I am torn apart by my many conflicting desires.

Changing for the better means sorting out my values,

prioritizing them, and so choosing what kind of person I want to become.

I am created to become free, to become a lover, to become a builder of the Kingdom. This is not automatic! If this is to happen, then, under the grace of the Spirit, I must become free; I must learn to love unselfishly; I must learn to become an instrument of peace and not war. I must grow, change for the better. This is what conversion is about.

Yes, "Be gentle with me; I'm not done yet!"

CHAPTER FIVE

All of Me Is Me!

In the last chapter I sought to highlight my oneness as a human person. In the past I tended to drive a wedge between body and soul, to see them as separate and more or less unconnected. Now I am aware that while I can mentally distinguish body and soul, the two function as one.

In this chapter I want to look at several basic aspects of my oneness. The Spirit helps me follow Jesus through all aspects of my life. Nothing about me is alien or foreign to the touch of grace. "All of me is me." God is with me in all I am. The spiritual life embraces the whole of my life.

I want to dwell on this from five different perspectives. I am bodily, sensual, emotional, sexual, spiritual. God's gracious love touches me in all aspects of my being. In coming to appreciate and accept each of these aspects I discover Jesus, and grow in my spiritual life.

As I look at these five aspects of who I am, I see them precisely as orienting me to others. All of them enable me to be in relation with others, to come to union with others and ultimately with God.

For example, my sexuality is not just an aspect of me that affects me as an individual. Sexuality touches my whole being as a person; it reveals my incompleteness; it brings out the fact that I am made for relationships; I am made for union with others.

I Am Bodily

Notice I say "I am bodily," not "I have a body." The language here is significant. To say "I have a body" is like saying I have a red Oldsmobile; I possess it. It is not me.

Referring to our bodiliness in that way promotes the separation of body and soul and detracts from the unity of the human person. I don't really "have" a body. My body is me, as much as my soul is me. I am bodily.

I was blessed by God with good health and bodily strength. As a farmboy, I was proud of my bodily strength. I was proud of doing "manly" work by the time I was ten. In high school I was even more conscious of my bodily strength and coordination and my abilities in various sports. I gloried in being able as a freshman to hold my own with the seniors, to show them I was as strong and tough as they.

Looking back I know I valued myself, felt good about myself, found much of my worth in what I was able to do because of my bodily capacities.

The ironic twist in this was that in other ways I failed to appreciate myself as bodily. I failed to appreciate my senses, my feelings and my sexuality. I identified these with the body. I "have" senses, feelings, sexuality. I separated myself from them. I didn't look upon them as "spiritual."

I took my body for granted. I did not appreciate my health, my strength. I even mistreated my body. My participation in violent sports, taking unnecessary risks, bad eating habits, smoking, bad working habits, poor posture, etc.—all involved a lack of respect for my body.

For a long time I have been struggling to appreciate and to be grateful for my body. I even seek to rejoice in being bodily. I seek to find the balance, the harmony, of myself as *both* bodily *and* spirit.

Some of my efforts have borne fruit: I look at my body and feel it in a more reverent and respectful way, though I am still somewhat embarrassed to look at myself. I am more grateful for my body, my health, my strength and all the incredible things I am able to do because I am bodily. I take better care of my health now. I watch my diet. I stopped smoking. I am more gentle with my body. I am also more thankful for my senses: the wonder of seeing, hearing, touching, smelling, tasting.

I appreciate more the incredible capacity to feel anger,

desire, affection, gentleness, fear, love. I reach out to others, greet them with a hug, say good-bye with a kiss. I have begun to discover body language, the joy of reaching out and touching someone.

What is so marvelous in all this incarnational development is that I've come to appreciate myself more and to find Jesus in new ways. I believe more deeply and realistically than ever that "The Word was made flesh, and dwelt among us," that Jesus was bodily as I am, that it's OK to be bodily. My spiritual life is much richer because it is more solidly based in the truth that I am a bodily person.

I Am a Sensual Person

Not too many years ago I wouldn't dare say I was sensual. That word had bad implications. As a sensual person, presumably I was giving in too much to my senses, which would lead me into temptation. I learned that God created us with five senses, but.... The senses were OK, but...my senses could betray me, seduce me, deceive me. I learned to guard my senses, to keep custody of them.

1) Don't look! As a student and seminarian, I was warned to be careful what I looked at. I should not look into the eyes of others. I should keep my eyes downcast. I should not look at girls or women, not even pictures of them. Most especially I was not to look at people or pictures that showed nudity.

When I look back, this all seems so strange. God created people and things in such incredible beauty, but it was so dangerous (an occasion of sin) to behold such beauty. A funny God!

It should be noted that what I learned is not necessarily what I was taught. (Any teacher knows that.) My teachers had a valid concern: Our senses could open up avenues that could be spiritually dangerous.

They were trying to teach me to appreciate and make use of my senses wisely and prudently. So eager were they to impress this on my young mind that they exaggerated, and I went away with the impression that the senses were all bad and to be rigidly controlled.

It took me a long time to recognize and overcome this denial of my humanness, to realize what a gift sight is, not only for reading and study, but especially to look at, to gaze at another person. I behold such wondrous beauty all around me and discover Jesus in all I see.

I came to understand the incredible request of the blind beggar in the Gospel: "Lord, that I may see." I discovered the gift of seeing what appears outwardly as the medium through which I am able to see inwardly into the meaning of events, experiences, relationships, myself. Ultimately the insight of faith leads me even to the vision of God in human persons and human events.

In the Scriptures I find the powerful themes of darkness and light, blindness and seeing, sin and grace. Jesus has come to lead me out of darkness into the light. Baptism is the sacrament of illumination. All through life, I seek to see and to understand. I long to gain insight into the meaning of my life. I deeply desire to see God through the light of faith. I pray to Jesus: "Lord, that I may see."

2) **Don't touch!** Another lesson I learned early in life was "Don't touch." I took for granted that it was another strange way to become "holy." It was another confirmation that the spiritual life had little to do with our ordinary human life. Very nonincarnational!

"Don't touch" is even harder, in a way, than "don't look." I could keep my eyes cast down yet snatch a little peek, but I found that not touching almost required getting outside my own skin. When I heard, "Don't touch babies. Don't touch boys. Don't touch girls. Don't touch any other person. Don't touch yourself. Don't touch animals," I didn't know what to make of it.

Naturally and instinctively I touched, and then felt guilty. I touched, and then was accused of being sensual. I touched, and felt hostile to my own body. I was mixed up!

Gradually, I dared to touch. I discovered the wonder of touch. I could feel the texture of wood, marble, cloth. I could feel warmth and cold, rough and smooth. I could feel skin, hair, bones. I could hold another person's hand and speak volumes without words. I could embrace a person in pain and communicate what words could not. I could kiss another with a tenderness that no other gesture could express.

What was so marvelous in this discovery was the deepening awareness that in coming to appreciate the sense of touch, I was becoming more aware of my whole self. I increasingly valued my relationships and I was seeing new aspects of family and community. My world took on new meaning.

In all this, through faith, I came to know and follow Jesus in wondrous new ways. In his miracles, in the way he was with others, he helped me discover touch—and so to discover him!

I was also learning to perceive the evil and violence, the hurt and devastation, that can be caused through touch. I can hit and harm. I can kill by physical touch. I can "kill" through emotional violence and verbal abuse, which at times can be even more painful than physical abuse.

As I get older, I realize I need to reach out and touch others. This is true for everyone, from infancy on. It is especially true for older persons who often experience terrible loneliness.

Touching is critical to interpersonal relations, human intimacy. There is no substitute. We may not be able to see or hear or taste or smell, but if there is no sense of touch, then it seems we are dead.

In my family touching was quite rare. Indeed for years it was practically nonexistent, except for hitting in ways that hurt. I remember in later years I hugged my dad, my brothers and sister, even learned to kiss them, and so expressed my love in new and more powerful ways. This has come to mean so much to me.

One day in a museum I saw a statue which, instead of the usual "don't touch," had a very attractive sign that read: "Please touch!" That's the sign God intended in the whole of creation, especially in the world of human persons: "Please touch." When God created us and saw that it was good, he put out a sign for everyone: "Please touch!" "Taste and see the goodness of the Lord."

I could reflect in a similar way about hearing, tasting,

smelling. Each of these, too, enables me to be in touch with my self, my world, the events of my life, and especially with others.

I believe that I am created by God to be a sensual person. I am flesh and blood as well as mind and heart. I would be much more appreciative and respectful of others if I were more in touch with the functioning of my senses. I would love others more realistically and healthily if I were generally more in tune with myself as a bodily and sensual person. My senses open me to the human and so to God. That's incarnational spirituality.

I Am a Feeling Person

In my early years, especially in my teens, I tried hard to do what was expected of me and hardly ever got out of line. I wanted to be a "good guy." I wanted to succeed. I wanted the approval of my teachers and those in authority. I would not allow my feelings to surface; I bottled up any feelings that might get me in trouble.

Anger was the only feeling that I was aware of. On rare occasions when I did express anger, it was a small explosion, and usually came out inappropriately. Other feelings seldom surfaced and were quickly suppressed.

From my own experience and the experiences others have shared with me in my retreat work and spiritual direction, I have become convinced that the biggest obstacle to spiritual growth for most people is failure to face and deal well with their feelings, especially anger.

I have great difficulty with anger. Often I act as though I'm not angry and even say I'm not angry. I don't recognize my anger; I try to "stuff" my anger; I don't know how to express anger constructively; I'm afraid of anger. But, then, I'm afraid of all my feelings.

The greatest challenge of my life is to love other people. Nothing stifles my loving others so much as my inability or unwillingness to communicate. Nothing so hinders me from communicating so much as my inability and/or my unwillingness to share my feelings (without attacking or doing violence to others), and my inability to respect the feelings of others. I share so much more fully when I dare to share my feelings.

I grew up quite out of touch with my feelings. I paid little attention to what I felt or what others felt. Feelings were of little account. Feelings were embarrassing and only got you into trouble. Ideas, issues—these were important.

When I first felt the need to get in touch with my feelings, I read a lot. Psychology was being brought to bear on religious formation and on spiritual growth and development. This gave me some insights that aided me in doing my "homework."

I found it difficult to deal constructively with my feelings in my relationships with others. I was communicative in the realm of ideas, but on a more personal level, I could not communicate. I had learned to listen fairly well, but I could not share my feelings.

In many ways I did not even know what I felt, much less how to express my feelings without dumping or exploding. My tendency was to become silent, to withdraw, to close the door, to hide my feelings. Even today, after years of struggling, I still freeze when angry. I'm afraid of my feelings.

But I have made some progress in entering into my humanness, in getting in touch with my feelings. At times (though rarely!) I can even allow myself to cry. Every effort I have made, every little bit of progress under God's grace, has borne much fruit for me and for others, for my personal life and for my ministry.

Over the years I developed my own method of trying to deal with my feelings. First, I identify what I am feeling. This is not easy. There are so many different kinds of feelings, so many different ways I feel in given situations, and often I feel many different things at the same time. But, if I can name what I feel, I begin to feel liberated. The feeling is no longer overwhelming. I have a chance to move gracefully.

Second, I appreciate what I am feeling. Why do I feel the way I do? What prompted me to feel this way? I try to appreciate the legitimacy of the feeling. In trying to appreciate what I am feeling, I seek to remain factual. I do not want to moralize my feelings, to see some feelings as good and others as bad or unacceptable.

Third, I accept my feelings. This is the hardest thing for me. For so many years I looked down on my feelings as beneath me, as baby stuff, as unmanly, as out of place in someone who wants to be holy. To accept my feelings, to admit them, to claim them—that I find difficult.

But I believe this is the only way to go. I believe strongly in an incarnational spiritual life. I believe we do not grow in grace if we reject our humanness. And if we do not deal well with our feelings, we reject our humanness.

The gospel command is: Love God; love one another. I no longer see how we can fulfill this command if we do not learn to accept, respect and deal in a healthy way with our feelings.

I Am a Sexual Person

Another important way in which I do not accept my humanness is the way I have failed to accept and appreciate my sexuality.

This is not surprising in light of my history. I had difficulty accepting my body and my feelings. I was strongly influenced by the negative approach to sexuality when I was growing up.

From what others of all walks of life have shared with me, I know my experience was not unusual. In some ways other Christian denominations were more negative and more rigid than Catholics. The "puritanical blight" affected our culture and most everyone in it.

In the mid-seventies I taught a course on the moral and spiritual dimensions of human sexuality to about fifty students of five different Christian denominations. Everyone without exception spoke of this negative approach to sexuality. They all indicated that they had had practically no sexual education at home or church or school. It's not surprising that the lid finally blew off.

I remember little of any kind of instruction concerning sexuality at home or school before, during or after my teens. The subject was never brought up. The few remarks that were made were mostly negative, warning about behavior that was forbidden, acts against the sixth and ninth commandments.

In general, people seemed to assume I knew all I needed to know about sexuality, and I certainly did not feel welcome to ask questions. Mostly what instruction I did receive dealt with all the ways people could do evil and why every single act of impurity was a *big* sin.

When I took some initiative and went to the library, the only books available were on marriage, and they had little or nothing to say positively about sexuality or the virtue of chastity, even in marriage.

What does all this say about the Good God who created us as sexual persons: "Male and female he created them, and he saw that it was good!" As one person put it, "God really blew it!" The negative, pessimistic and legalistic impressions I received were, sadly, all too prevalent.

When in college, I read a book by Dietrich von Hildebrand, entitled *In Defense of Purity*. It was a most unusual book for the forties because it presented purity in a positive and attractive way. What saddens me is that I felt it was just too good to be true. The beautiful and positive message of the author got lost, smothered by the negative impressions I had received.

For a long time I also felt I was the only one who felt this way about sexuality. As I got older, and especially through my ministry in the confessional and parlor, I realized that practically everyone at some time in their lives struggles with sexuality.

So many experience sexuality with anxiety, fear, guilt. Most seem confused as to what to make of it, as to what sexuality really means. Many feel that purity is the most important thing in their lives, and so feel great guilt whenever they fail in the slightest way. Many are caught up in frustration and hopelessness. How could something so beautiful and good, so pervasive of our whole being, our experiences, our relationships, become so deadly, so fearsome?

I remember well a middle-aged husband and father who felt so guilty when he felt attracted to a beautiful woman, not his wife. A young wife felt guilty because she was terribly embarrassed to be seen naked by her husband. An elderly widow missed her husband so much and felt guilty because she powerfully longed for intercourse with him, and was aroused when she felt this. I remember the teenagers struggling with the burden of guilt because they had stimulated themselves genitally. So many people felt impure and guilty because of ordinary human sexual feelings, sensations and desires. God only knows the terrible damage done, the fear and guilt induced, because almost everyone thought the mere occurrence of "bad thoughts" was a sin.

Gradually I realized that what is best in our Catholic tradition looks upon sexuality in a positive way. Our tradition is rooted in the fact that God created us male and female. God wanted us to be sexual. And God saw that it was *good*! Jesus entered fully into our human condition. Jesus became a sexual human being. It is good to be sexual! Somehow, this beautiful teaching did not greatly influence my approach to human sexuality.

Slowly I realized that my sexuality is relational, that I am made for union with others, for intimacy. Intimacy for humans is impossible without the sexual aspect—who I am as a man or woman—being involved. The gospel call to love my neighbor cannot be fulfilled in an angelic way, as a disembodied spirit. I can only love others if I do so as a human person, as a sexual person.

I saw that the virtue of chastity cannot be understood merely as a list of do's and don'ts. Purity is a virtue, a power, a grace, that enables me to come to know, understand, appreciate and accept my sexuality as a dimension of my whole being and so incorporate and integrate it into my Christian life.

This awakening to the meaning of sexuality did *not* bring about the growth I sought in my life. Growth in becoming pure is far more than knowing about purity. Yet, it is an important and graceful beginning.

At least I had some idea of the work I needed to do with the grace of God. I prayed as never before to the Holy Spirit to enlighten me, to guide me, to inspire me, to empower me to begin to accept myself, to enable me to begin to live chastely.

Once, a woman shared with me, with great difficulty, her struggle to remain pure. She sobbed as she admitted how she had fallen. Almost overcome with shame and guilt, she expressed her great desire to be pure and indicated her efforts to remain pure. She wanted with all her heart to love God. She wondered how God could forgive her!

As I listened to this woman, heard the goodness of her heart, felt her profound desire to be pure, I said to her: "I wish I could tell you, show you, how pure you are. I wish I could tell you how pleasing you are to God."

She could hardly believe me. We talked about how purity is the virtue (power, grace) that calls us to struggle to become pure. She came to see, and find courage, in the fact that her struggles to become more pure were an expression of the virtue of purity. She had failed, but far more she had succeeded. She could even sense that Jesus was with her in her struggles. What a difference this made in this woman's life.

I Am a Spiritual Person

Earlier I touched on my oneness as a human person. I had difficulty experiencing body and soul as one. They seemed to be at odds.

It seemed my ordinary day-to-day activities and experiences, which obviously involved my body, my senses and my feelings, had little or nothing to do with my spiritual life. Real spiritual activities, real spiritual exercises, were few and far between.

For example, this separation of the spiritual from the ordinary, the human, was implied in the whole matter of distractions in prayer. Can any human person try to pray and not experience distractions? It's the way the mind, the imagination, the memory work! Yet, distractions in prayer were considered sinful, at least an imperfection. Somehow this symbolizes just how inhuman and nonincarnational our spirituality had become.

I remember vividly another woman I met while in spiritual direction. Out of the blue I was struck with the realization: She's telling me about her difficulties and struggles to be a good mother to her three small children. She's telling me about her spiritual life! She's telling me about her life with God. She's revealing God in her life, and all the while she's talking about changing diapers, cleaning, cooking and being patient with screaming kids. It hit me hard: That's the spiritual life. That's incarnational spirituality.

I remember for years hearing people talk about experiencing God. I didn't know what they were talking about. I had not had these experiences of God, at least none that I recognized. All I ever had were ordinary human, flesh and blood, experiences. I didn't experience God in prayer. At least it didn't feel like it.

Then, one day I discovered anew a prayer of Saint Francis, called "Praises of God." In this prayer, Francis says to God:

> You are love, charity. You are wisdom; You are humility;
> You are patience; You are beauty; You are meekness;
> You are security; You are inner peace; You are joy; You
> are our hope; You are justice; You are moderation...

It hit me! I have experienced tenderness, justice, love, patience, moderation. I have experienced beauty, inner peace. I have experienced these "goods" in persons, in situations, in events. They were ordinary experiences. But, Saint Francis says, they are also experiences of God.

Francis is saying that God is *good*, all good, and God is the source of all good. Whenever I experience any kind of goodness, in any form or shape, I am experiencing God. That's incarnational spirituality!

Slowly, it dawns on me: The spiritual life is not inhuman, opposed to the human. The spiritual life is not some esoteric, disembodied, unfeeling, insensate sort of life. The spiritual life is the flesh and blood, ordinary life of a person insofar as she or he is touched and moved by the grace of the Holy Spirit. I experience God in the here and now.

I can say, then, that I am spiritual and not deny my bodiliness. I can be spiritual at the same time I am bodily, sensual, emotional, intellectual, volitional. Indeed, for me as a human person, I can only be spiritual precisely as human, precisely as enfleshed spirit. In this light I could understand the married lady who once told me that one of the most spiritual moments in her life occurred while she was having genital intercourse with her husband.

I am spiritual as a human person because I am led by the Spirit, moved by God's love, touched by grace. When I say "I am spiritual," not only am I not denying my humanness in any aspect, I am affirming that all aspects of me, all my experiences as a human person, are open to the Spirit.

One big way I came to realize I am spiritual was through the gospel command to love: to love God above all, with my whole being and with my whole heart. That is the spiritual life. That is spiritual activity. That is not possible if I deny my humanness, my very self. I can only love God through the grace of the Spirit (spiritually). I can only love God as God wishes when I love with my whole being, my whole heart, my whole human reality.

It follows inevitably that I must love my neighbor, every other person, with my whole being, with my whole heart. I cannot truthfully say I love God (whom I cannot see) if I don't love my neighbor (whom I do see). Nor can I love God with my whole being, if I do not love my neighbor with my whole heart, my whole self, all my human capacities (body, soul, senses, feelings).

When I say "I am spiritual," I mean getting down to the nitty-gritty stuff of daily living. I am spiritual when I clean my room. I am spiritual when I try to be understanding of another person's situation. I am spiritual when I listen with mercy to someone who is asking for forgiveness.

When I wrestle with failing health and whether to accept unusual treatment, I am spiritual. When I clean the bathroom, read a book, give a talk, watch TV, take a walk, fix a flat, have a drink, smell a flower, hold a baby, hug a friend, I am spiritual. When I cry, go to church, pray the rosary, I am spiritual.

In all my intellectual pursuits; in my efforts to know, understand, plan; in all my efforts to develop and care for our world; in all my relationships with technology, communications, media, travel, outer (and inner) space, education, health care, justice and penal systems, I am spiritual.

I am spiritual because the Holy Spirit graces me in my humanness. The Spirit is with me, and, mysteriously, nurtures and quickens me, especially in my human capacity to become free. The Spirit moves me to express my very self in free choices, yet does not determine my choices. In a way I am most God-like, most spiritual, and yet most human, when I express myself in making free choices.

In my free choices (insofar as they are free and moved by grace) I am creating, shaping my very self, my life, my relationships with others. My family, community, society, world calls me to responsibility; I am responsible when I make free choices, choices that are mine. In and through my daily choices I am shaping my response to God's love. I am fashioning my relationship to God.

In sum, the most mysterious and wondrous aspect of being spiritual, of being moved by the Spirit, is my capacity as a human person to go beyond the here and now. As a spiritual person, and through my free choices, I am able to transcend my material boundaries. I am able to reach out and touch others.

I am able to be sensitive, sympathetic, compassionate. I am able to respect, appreciate, affirm, care for others. I can hear words spoken by another and understand the other's meaning. I can speak words and touch another's spirit. I am able to experience ecstasy, not only the extraordinary ecstasies of some of the saints, but the ordinary, human moments when I am pulled out of myself—by a beautiful sunset, the power of the ocean, the touch of a friend. Indeed, holiness is wholeness!

CHAPTER SIX

I Do Not Walk Alone

My whole endeavor in this book is to explore ways in which
God is present and working in my daily life. More and more I
want to discover the divine dimension of my ordinary human
experience. This is the mystery of the Incarnation: the word of
God enfleshed, dwelling in our midst. The Kingdom of God is
within you!

This gives meaning to the human "stuff" of life. Human
history is indeed salvation history. All created reality is
"sacrament," revealing God. My personal life is pregnant with
divine possibilities. This means my daily life is no longer
boring; the humdrum becomes exciting; the ordinary is
unusual. God is with us, in Jesus, in every moment and facet of
life.

In Acts (10:36-38) Peter said to Cornelius and the people in
his house: "You know...how God anointed Jesus of Nazareth
with the Holy Spirit and power. He went about doing good and
healing all those oppressed by the devil, for God was with
him."

This is the story of our life, our very human life in Christ. It
is precisely as human persons that we are anointed by God with
the Holy Spirit and power (Baptism and Confirmation). In
Jesus we are to go about doing good works. We are to love in
ways that touch and heal the hearts of the people we meet, work
with, live with. And we marvel that in Jesus, God is with us!

In these pages, I've reflected on this in many ways in terms
of who I am as a created human person. I have pondered this
mystery of incarnation in terms of my unity, depth and
development as a person. I've tried to see, through faith, that
God is present and at work in all of me, in all I am: bodily,

sensual, emotional, sexual, spiritual.

Now, I come to further mystery. I do not live, or walk, alone. My whole existence is bound up with others (relationships). My whole life is embedded in the social fabric of human existence (family, society).

I am relational; as a person I can knowingly and lovingly turn to another, communicate, share hopes and dreams, life itself. I am created to be in relation with others.

I am social. I am not just involved in a series of disconnected relationships. My whole existence is caught up in the wondrous web of connected relationships. The sum of these relationships bind me simultaneously into a union with many other persons. They are at the heart of who I am and who I come to be. For better or worse, my whole being, and all my living, is situated, even embedded and rooted, in family, society and world.

This is the way God wanted it to be. This is God's intention. It is God's desire, inherent in our nature as human persons. "It is not good for men and women to be alone" (see Genesis 2:18-25). God's gracious plan for human history is fulfilled in Jesus (see Ephesians 1:10). In Jesus, I am called to reflect Trinitarian life: a unique person so deeply caught up in knowing and loving others that we become one. I am meant for union. I do not walk alone.

I Am Relational

It is embarrassing to say that for a long time I was quite aware of being an individual, but being relational was not very important to me. In fact I even avoided relationships of any depth.

Of course I was aware of other people, and, in some rather superficial ways, I related to them. But, "other people" were primarily those who were older, in charge, in authority; they were the ones I had to obey. Those my own age, or younger, were not that important to me. I was comfortable being alone.

In high school I never got close to anyone. I sought in every way to be obedient to my elders. With my peers I competed so as to come out on top. (Then, those in authority would be proud of me.) I got along with others but never related with any sort of depth or mutuality.

As I look back, two factors stand out that explain this. First, I grew up on a farm and spent much time on my own, out in the fields, working alone, etc. I became very self-reliant.

I prided myself that I could stand on my own two feet, that I didn't need anyone, that I could do it myself. When I was with my peers in school, I was always in a competitive situation. I struggled to be "first" in all my schoolwork.

Second, I tended to be quiet, shy, inward. I was not inclined to open myself to friendship, to any relationship that was more than superficial. I was afraid because I was ignorant about myself and had no idea what was inside me, what sort of person I was. I was also afraid that if others got to know me, they would not like me.

Whatever the reasons, the fact is I can look back on my life and see that I was very much a loner. I didn't want anyone to get close to me.

My early history makes this somewhat understandable. I left home, the farm in Kansas, when I was only thirteen and went to Cincinnati, a city filled with strangers, to attend the Franciscans' high school seminary. From age thirteen until I was ordained at age twenty-six, I hardly knew anyone but boys and men. My life was spent in a tightly structured living situation. Relationships were quite superficial. Indeed, "particular friendships" were frowned upon.

My early experience may be somewhat unique and different from most teenagers'. But I've come to believe that, whatever be the situations in which they grew up, almost everyone has real difficulties in appreciating the meaning and importance of deep relationships. Studies show that most people find it difficult to sustain deep, mutual relationships, especially men. Men are strongly influenced by culture and become macho, chauvinistic and afraid to share their feelings. I was no different than many men.

Being in relationship with others is the most important aspect of our lives as humans and as gospel persons. The absolute demand of the gospel to love neighbor means entering into relationships with other men and women. All grace moves us to love one another, to relate lovingly (justly, truthfully, purely) with each other. Grace moves us always in the direction of friendship.

My vow of chaste celibacy not only demanded that I avoid certain forms of genital sexual behavior, but more positively, it demanded that I become a loving person, able to relate to others in a loving way.

Indeed this is true of every person, single, celibate, married. I must refrain from any sexual genital behavior inconsistent with my state in life. But, I am challenged to grow in my ability to relate to others in a loving and healthy way.

How to begin? Relationships don't just happen. Once some initial movements occur in a ministerial setting, a social setting, or the like, relationships need gentle, reverent, unhurried caring. Sometimes they develop; sometimes they don't. Something graceful and mysterious is at stake.

Relationships cannot be forced. The most important disposition is to dare to be open. I need to be open to the possibility of relationships that are personal, something more than a simple working relationship, more than casual acquaintance.

Relationships will not develop if I continue to give the signal, "Don't come close to me," or if I continue to be closed and unwilling to share myself. Relationships demand not only that I share my thoughts and ideas, but that I even dare to share a little of my feelings, hopes and dreams, aches and sorrows, shame and embarrassments, weakness and sinfulness.

I found this scary and extremely difficult. I wanted such relationships, but that wasn't enough! I gradually had to face the awful fact that in many ways I was incapable of such relationships through deep, ingrained habits of aloofness, individualism and the need to be in control.

I was afraid of losing control. I felt so vulnerable. I was vaguely conscious of so much in me, in my life and in my background, that I was ashamed of. I was fearful that this would come out. I was afraid to face it and even more afraid to share it.

But somehow by the grace of God, when I dared to want

70

better and more personal relationships in my life, when I began, at least a little, to be open to the remote possibility that someone else might just care a little for me, things began to happen and some persons began to touch me deeply.

I was amazed; I was moved! I was scared to death, yet fascinated. I began to be happy in a way I had never known. The world began to look different, better. My vocation became more precious than ever. My fellow friars never looked so good. My ministry seemed to become more fruitful. My prayer became more real. I actually began to relate to Jesus in a more human way and talked to him about my growing up!

I fell into two traps. First, I read and read in the area of relationships. I slowly became able to talk about relationships, deep personal sharing, friendship, communication, etc., and I somehow assumed that because I could talk about all this, I was able to *do* it. That simply was not true, but it took me years to realize my mistake. Meanwhile, I betrayed, pushed away and hurt the very people I cared for.

Second, I fell into the trap of thinking that because I was a good listener, because I could respect another person who shared deeply with me, I could relate well. I took it for granted that because I could accept the other persons in whatever they shared, because I could understand through my listening and assist them in discovering the faith meaning of their experiences, I could relate deeply.

I unwittingly thought that because I developed these ministerial skills in spiritual direction and counseling that I was becoming quite adept at relating to others. How presumptuous and how wrong.

I seemed to be unaware of the one-sidedness in my relationships. All the while I gloried in those relationships and even supposed them to be mutual. Yet I hardly ever shared much about my self and what I was really feeling, at least in any deeply personal way.

I also placed other roadblocks in the path of my growing in the ability to relate. In my fear of going overboard in developing friendships, in my fear of losing my vocation because of developing friendships with women, I deliberately put limits and conditions (very one-sidedly, I must say) on these relationships.

My ministry would always come first. If there was any time or opportunity left, then I would give attention to my friends. As one friar put it, "I came to live with you because I thought we were friends. Now that we live in the same house, I find I need an appointment to get to see you!" I put so many limits on my friends, it is a wonder they all didn't just walk away.

I made progress. I also made terrible mistakes. I brought lots of pain to people. I proceeded in ways that were often proud and conceited. I could be, unconsciously, disrespectful. I was at times so angry as to become violent, destructive and downright evil. I could be so chauvinistic, so demanding and domineering!

At times I was guilty of just about everything that could go wrong in a relationship. As I look back, I benefited greatly from the experiences I had, even with all my bungling. I pray God (and those I've betrayed) to forgive me for ways I offended others, who looked to me for so much and received so little. I beg God to forgive me for all the ways I hurt, manipulated and took advantage of others.

In what time I have left, I hope and pray I grow in relating to my friends, to beg forgiveness of those I've hurt or betrayed. I want to incarnate the love of Jesus in my human and personal and graceful relationships with others.

I Am Social

William Barry, in *Paying Attention to God*, writes: "We humans live not only in an intra- and interpersonal world but also in a world of social, political, cultural and religious institutions, structures and ambience that condition everything we experience and do."

Inculturation. We are born and reared in our culture; we are profoundly affected by our culture; we are enculturated through and through; and we're hardly aware of it. According to Barry, "Many of these cultural expectations and values are contrary to Christian values and hopes, but they also are so ingrained in us that we are often not even aware that we have them."

I am who I am, I grow as a person, I relate to others, in the midst of my history, my culture. I am rooted, deeply sunk, completely permeated by my culture. The culture into which I am born and raised touches me in every fiber of my being. My emotions, my attitudes, my value system, and so my choices and behavior, are deeply influenced by my culture.

Again, Barry writes:

> ...educated, middle-class Americans share many unarticulated cultural values and expectations. Body odors are anathema, for example. Running hot water, three square meals a day, with snacks in between, a relatively full refrigerator and larder, T.V. and a car at one's disposal or at least available for use through negotiation, money for movies and other entertainment, these are only a few of the expectations middle-class Americans share. We expect that hard work will be rewarded and tend to assume that lack of such rewards results from laziness. We accept what social scientists call the "just world hypothesis" and thus tend to presume that the victims of calamities such as rape, a mutilating accident or endemic poverty are somehow responsible for their plight.

In light of all I've experienced and tried to express in this book, I believe I discover and experience God in the human. My spiritual life is profoundly affected by my inculturation. God comes to me—a farmboy from Kansas. God loves me as I grew up ploughing Kansas soil with a team of mules. God calls me by name—a thirteen-year-old farm kid who gloried in brawn and brains and little else.

God touches me with all my values and prejudices, with my history of independence and strength, violence and fears, hard work and pride, poverty and rich potential.

This is the stuff in which Jesus leads me in mystery and grace, the place and time of divine invitation to "more," to what is not yet. This concrete socio-cultural-history is loaded with the possible shape of my future. God is present to me as enculturated. In the here and now God seeks to bring me to life in Christ, to shape me into becoming a more mature person, a better Christian, a truer Friar Minor.

Socialization. Vatican II speaks of our socialization in the document *The Church in the Modern World*: "Man's social nature makes it evident that the progress of the human person and the advance of society itself hinge on each other. From the beginning, the subject and the goal of all social institutions is and must be the human person, which for its part and by its very nature stands completely in need of social life. This social life is not something added on to man."

God is Trinity. God is three distinct and unique persons. These three persons are so in relation to each other: knowing and being known, loving and being loved, giving and receiving...so deeply, intimately, completely in relation to each other that these three persons are altogether one God. These three divine persons are completely and totally community.

Person, relations (love), community: As a human person that is my being, my living, my call, my destiny. I am made in God's image and likeness. I am a unique human person. As such I am capable of and made to be in relation to other persons. I am created to love and be loved (and all this implies) in such a way, in such depth, in such mutuality, that I become one with others. As a person I am called not only to relate to individual others. I am called to be a member of society; I am called to be family.

Interpersonal relations are important, not only in themselves. They are important because they are the stuff out of which communities are formed, out of which society takes shape. Family, society (Church, state), community—that is the goal of our living.

The night before he died for us, Jesus prayed that we might live in unity: "...so that all may be one, as you, Father, are in me and I in you, that they also may be in us, that the world may believe that you sent me" (John 17:21). This unity can only come about when we love one another in a way that blossoms forth in social justice and peace.

In the Gospel Jesus put all this much more bluntly: "This is how all will know that you are my disciples, if you have love for one another" (John 13:35). Love (and the justice, truth, purity that love demands) is the only way I can relate that unites me with others. All forms of behavior that are not loving tear us apart, divide us, alienate us, separate us.

Love moves me to respect, appreciate and accept others. Hatred moves me to self-seeking and all forms of violence, culminating in killing and murder. Love moves me to be responsible for others, to care for, to stand by others. Hatred drives me into going my own way, uninterested, uncaring, or worse, exploiting others.

Love draws me to forgiveness and reconciliation. Hatred erupts in quarreling, fighting, warfare. Love moves me close to others, seeking ways of justice and peace. Hatred moves me apart, seeking ways of vengeance. Love moves me to respect our differences yet binds our hearts together. Hatred boils over into prejudice, disrespectful stereotypes, envy, jealousy, rivalries, manipulation, discrimination, domination. Love moves me to respect my enemies and find ways of peace. Hatred moves me to kill my enemies and find ways of ever greater destruction.

The gospel demands social justice. I am my brother's and sister's keeper. I am responsible for the world, for all humans. I self-destruct when I turn my back on my brothers and sisters.

Vatican II affirms: "God did not create us for life in isolation, but for the formation of social unity. So also 'it has pleased God to make us holy and save us not merely as individuals, without any mutual bonds, but by making us into a single people, a people which acknowledges Him in truth and serves Him in holiness' " (*The Church in the Modern World*, #31).

I commit spiritual and moral suicide when I refuse to get involved in society and seek ways of being helpful. I thwart God's plan and harm God's image; I betray myself when I try to go it alone, when I seek to avoid involvement in issues of social justice, economic justice, political issues.

I deny my very self when I don't care about the poor, the outcast, the downtrodden. I betray the fabric of my being when

I don't do what I can to help everyone have opportunities for education, health care, home, employment. I blind myself to my destiny as a social being when I don't seek to transcend my self and be there for others.

I've always felt it was vitally important to do God's will, but I understood this mostly in terms of law: To do God's will I had to obey all the law, and do what others commanded. Gradually I began to see that there is much more to life than what "laws" can encompass. My life is much bigger than obedience to laws. I must do God's will in a much deeper, fuller sense.

God calls me to freedom, to grow and take responsibility for my whole life and all my actions. God calls me to love my neighbors, all of them. God asks me to open my heart to other people, to relate to them, to care for them. God's absolute will is that I become a constructive member of the community, and spend my creative energies building community, becoming an instrument of peace.

God is terribly interested in and concerned about the world, every creature, all people, the human condition. Jesus gives meaning to the whole realm of creation, to the hearts and lives of every person.

Jesus invites us to love him by loving each other. Jesus invites us to care for him and so care for ourselves, by caring for our brothers and sisters, by addressing each other's hunger, thirst, nakedness, homelessness, imprisonment, alienation. Jesus calls us to build bonds, not barriers, to create unity not disunity.

Jesus is present—loving, forgiving, saving—not only in individual persons, not only in each interpersonal relationship, not only in each family and community. Jesus is present and working in the whole of human society to bring about God's Kingdom.

Jesus is present in all of society, in all social institutions, in all social structures and in all social systems. The goodness of God is revealed in our systems: education, welfare, health care, etc. In these and other structures and systems, the grace of God touches so many lives in so many ways.

But all these systems, structures, institutions, share in the human condition. They are not perfect. They are, in more or less serious ways, flawed, broken, evil. In real ways the very people these structures are designed to help are overlooked, left out, treated in inhuman ways, even oppressed. At the same time other people misuse these systems for their own gain. Our social institutions need redemption, and I must be involved in this process.

I jeopardize my spiritual well-being if I am not aware of, and involved in, the redemption of these structures. Jesus needs every one of us to be his instruments of peace. I dare not pick and choose with Jesus. I cannot love Jesus fully in Church if I don't try to love him in the person in the gutter. If following Jesus is to become real, I must hear his call to love all my brothers and sisters, especially the poor, the down-and-out.

If I only love and care for my own kind, if I love only those who think as I do, if I only love those who live the way I live, then I have not heard Jesus. I have not listened to the gospel. I have denied the Incarnation. The grace of the Spirit falls on my deaf ears.

Sometimes when I think about all the social-economic-political-cultural dimensions of following Jesus, I get discouraged. When I see the violence, the hurt, the destructive behavior all around me, I want to run away. When I become aware of corruption in politics, in business, of greed and corruption and injustice in the economic realm, I want to scream and climb in a hole. When I see the devastating results of addictions of all kinds, I want to tune it out and act as if it is not there. When I become aware of the tragedies of family life, the breakup of marriages, cruelty to children, sexual harassment, rape, vandalism, I want to yell "enough," and quit!

Jesus won't let me forget the cross, the power of love, the hope of the Spirit. Jesus reminds me that no matter how bad things get, there is a way out. It might not be an easy way, this way of death. It might not be attractive, this invitation to lay down my life for my brothers and sisters. At times I may not think they even deserve to be saved, but after all, who does? But laying down my life for others is the only way; as Jesus promised, it is the way to life, to victory, for everyone.

Yes, I am my brother's and sister's keeper. I do not love or walk alone. I may not have a scintillating social life, but I am a social person, whether I like it or not. I am all tangled up with other people. They won't leave me alone.

The power of evil is blatant and strong. But the power of grace is even stronger. Jesus is the first one who sang on Easter Sunday: "We shall overcome!" Incarnational spirituality is for real. We pray so often to "Our Father": "Thy Kingdom come, thy will be done on earth as in heaven." Taking this seriously will turn our hearts and lives inside out!

We do not walk alone!

[Note: To further explore this important topic, you might want to look for the following books: *Catholic Social Teaching: Our Best Kept Secret*, by P. J. Henriot, E. P. De Berri and M. J. Schultheis (Orbis Books, 1987), and *A Contemporary Spirituality* by F. X. Mechan (Orbis Books, 1984).]

CHAPTER SEVEN

'Now You See Me, Now You Don't!'

Several years ago I was privileged to spend two days on La Verna, the mountain in Italy so special to Saint Francis. It was here that Francis received the special grace of the stigmata, the experience of the wounds of Jesus in his own body.

In the Chapel of the Stigmata, there is a large three-dimensional scene of the crucifixion by the famous artist Della Robbia. While praying there I was struck by the depth of compassion of Mary and Francis. How deeply sensitive they were to the sufferings of Jesus. The question hit me: Why am I not more compassionate?

It struck me that my lack of compassion is largely due to my failure to admit my own vulnerability. The more I am closed to my vulnerability, the more I either do not see or am untouched by the sufferings of others. I become hardened to others; I lack compassion.

One way in which I refuse to admit my own vulnerability is by needing to be in control. I need to take charge, to run things, to dominate. I become aggressive, impatient, harsh and even violent. I want things to go my way. This need to control twists me out of shape. I become preoccupied with my own agenda. I am not open to others. I am not sensitive or compassionate to others.

Most of my life I've been involved in formation, supervision and spiritual direction. I learned that in these roles I needed to listen well but not get emotionally involved. I tried to show real concern and interest, but I sought to remain objective and professional. Thus I was in control. I did not allow myself to be vulnerable. I carried over this lack of emotional involvement into the rest of my life.

Similarly, in not accepting my own vulnerability, I found it hard to communicate. I would not let down my guard. I am adept at sharing intellectual ideas and opinions but not my feelings.

I see now this is detrimental to my relationships with others. Without struggling to promote open communication, I cannot do my share to build a relationship that is mutual. I cannot promote open communications if I am not ready to share my feelings and become vulnerable.

Lately, I have wondered why I have not gotten more personally involved in promoting social justice. I convinced myself that the best contribution I could make was in my teaching, spiritual direction and retreat ministry.

As I look back, I think I was afraid to expose my ignorance and weakness. I didn't want to get hurt, and I didn't want to change my life. I didn't want to open myself to ridicule, rejection, embarrassment—to be that vulnerable.

I think some of my fear of dying lies in my not accepting my vulnerability. I am afraid to take the first step in looking at my mortality. I am afraid to admit my frailty and limitations.

Past Spirituality

In the past I tended to focus on the Passion, the sufferings and death of Jesus and not a lot on the Resurrection. I knew I was to imitate Jesus in his sufferings. I was keenly aware that this life was a time of trials and tribulation, of pain and suffering. Resurrection, I tended to think, came at the end of the world.

With all this emphasis on suffering and the cross, I still didn't come to a sense of vulnerability. I practiced penance, mortification and self-denial. Yet, I didn't seem to enter into the meaning of my suffering. Somehow suffering seemed to come "from without"—from accidents or catching a cold or hurts caused by others. It didn't seem to get into my bones or seep into my heart that I am vulnerable in my very being as human, as creature, as a sinner.

More striking, I did not see my vulnerability in terms of my calling to love my neighbor. I am called to love, but I cannot love very well. I am called to relate, yet I cannot relate very deeply or intimately. I am called to mutuality but I feel the need to dominate or I sell out and become too submissive. To fulfill the law of love I must accept my vulnerability. This is precisely the way to new and risen life.

It is fearful and risky to be open, to let down my walls and barriers. It is painfully hard to entrust myself to others, to be open, to share my self and my feelings, my hopes and dreams, as well as my ideas and opinions. It's not easy to accept my vulnerability.

I Am Vulnerable

I am vulnerable simply because I am a creature; I am finite, limited, imperfect. When I eat too much I get a stomachache. It's the law of my nature. When I'm involved in some important work and miss a dinner with friends, I feel the pain of separation. I cannot be in two places at once. When I run out of time studying for a test and receive a B, I am disappointed. But I have only twenty-four hours in a day and only so much energy. I am vulnerable because I am limited.

I am a sinner. I know the sorrow and pain of moral evil, sinfulness. I try hard to be patient, but once in a while I fail. I experience my woundedness. I don't really want to be disrespectful, but sometimes I don't respect myself or others. I am vulnerable.

Just to be human is to be vulnerable, to be subject to sickness, disease, death. When I have a special trip planned and I wake up with the flu, when I get old and my muscles get flabby, I know I am vulnerable.

I can be hurt by my close friends, family members or fellow Franciscans, not because these people are mean or intend to hurt, but just because they are not perfect. They forget. They are thoughtless and careless. In this way, too, I experience my own vulnerability.

The Gospel Call

The gospel challenge to love others calls me to enter into my vulnerability, to accept my limitations, to admit that I am not perfect, to embrace my weakness, even my sinfulness. Therein I find Jesus and experience his saving and redemptive love.

Jesus, the Word made flesh, experienced vulnerability. Jesus knew what it meant to be limited, finite, weak and able to get hurt. Being born in a stable and laid in a manger is to know limits! Fleeing for his life into a foreign country is an experience of vulnerability.

All through his life, in all his experiences, Jesus knew limitations. He felt the pain of misunderstanding and ignorance and prejudice—even among his own disciples. Especially in his arrest, his trial and judgment, his passion and death, Jesus experienced the full force of vulnerability. Jesus experienced the final outcome of vulnerability: He died on a cross.

Two important things should be noted here. First, what gave meaning to Jesus' experience of vulnerability was his love for us. Jesus loved us. That's why he became human. Jesus loved us. That's why he became a creature—limited, finite, weak, powerless. Jesus loved us. That's why he entered fully into our human condition and experienced discouragement, disappointment, frustration, anger, pain and sorrow. Jesus loved us sinners and delivered himself up for us, even to death on a cross. Love is why he was willing to be so vulnerable.

Second, Jesus not only experienced hurt, pain, suffering, even death, with a heart full of love for us. *He rose from the dead.* Jesus opened himself in love to the full weight of vulnerability, and it cost him his life. But so complete was the obedient love of his heart that God raised him up. Jesus became a life-giving spirit.

I experience my vulnerability and death now with the hope and power of Jesus' love. I can hope that, in Jesus, I too shall overcome. In union with Jesus, vulnerability and death are not the last word. The last word is love and life: resurrection from the dead!

Jesus did not come to remove our vulnerability, to take away our suffering and sickness, to eliminate disease, tragedies and death. Jesus helps us accept being vulnerable.

Accepting my vulnerability keeps me from hardness of heart, rigidity and shutting others out. Instead of living in the fear of getting hurt, I can dare to accept my vulnerability as an aspect of being human that can open my heart to love and compassion. Thus, to hold in my arms a parent who just lost a child, to embrace someone who just found out he has cancer is to be vulnerable and become compassionate.

Jesus continues to be vulnerable in us, the members of his Body. When I enter into my own vulnerability and mortality, into my finiteness and our brokenness, I enter into the reality of my existence where the power of God is at work. For the same power of God that raised Jesus from the dead is at work in us, the Body of Christ, to bring us to fullness of risen life (see Ephesians 1:18-22).

The Experience of Dying = Mortality

Saint Francis had a wholesome sense of death. His Christian vision led him to embrace death as "sister." Death was not so much the terrible evil to be avoided and shunned at all cost; rather death became a friend, a sister, who would come to embrace us and ready us for a new beginning, a new life.

Saint Francis knew that death is not the end. He believed that Jesus, who died, is risen. Death is not our dreaded enemy; death is desirable sister. Death is not end; death is beginning. Death is not doomsday; death is birthday.

It might make a difference in my attitude if I stopped speaking of this critical moment of my life as "death" and began referring to it as my greatest "birthday."

This faith of Saint Francis, which opened his eyes to the Christian meaning of death, led him into the mystery of the Incarnation. Just as I don't know what it means to be human apart from Jesus, so I don't know what it means to be vulnerable, to be mortal, apart from Jesus. I don't know the meaning of death or the meaning of life apart from Jesus.

I hardly ever think of death. I don't want to think of it. I see death all around me, but somehow I don't think it will ever touch me. But sooner or later, in times of sickness or tragedy, I begin to sense that I too am going to die. This seems to be all the more true as I get older.

Our culture doesn't help; it even hinders. Our culture says in a thousand ways: "Death is the ultimate evil, the worst thing that can happen. Do everything in your power to avoid it, to stop it, to delay it."

Medicine has made incredible advances in the past seventy-five years. In our country life expectancy has steadily lengthened. Our lives can be prolonged in all kinds of ways. Organ transplants, even heart transplants, have become frequent. The intensive care units in our hospitals are loaded with the latest life-saving technology and know-how.

But this is a mixed blessing. The prolongation of life by extraordinary means can be a great blessing; it can be a tragedy. The frenzied effort to prolong life may be rooted in despair and give rise to untold misery to the sick person and the family.

There seems to be an assumption that we must do everything possible to avoid dying. The fear of lawsuits against doctors and hospitals has twisted us all out of shape. It not only adds greatly to medical surgical expenses, it has clouded and distorted our judgment.

We in our culture don't know what to feel about death. We don't want to talk about death. We don't want to be reminded of death. The cult of youth and beauty is irrational, rooted in fear. The paradox is that the more we run away from facing death, the more we tend to live in a way that hastens death (e.g., unhealthy eating and drinking habits, lack of exercise, drugs, etc.). Even our use of health and fitness centers can be motivated by an unbalanced fear of dying, a nonacceptance of our mortality.

The gospel is clear: I need to reckon with death, with my mortality, and to "seek the things that are above," to "lay up treasures in heaven." Otherwise I am the "deadest of the dead"; I am unable to experience death as birthday to new and lasting risen life.

In my journey to live a human life in Christ, I come to experience death and resurrection in the events and circumstances of daily life, in the ups and downs, the sorrows

84

and joys, the dyings and risings, of everyday living. Every human experience calls for some dying to self, to selfishness, to sin; at the same time every human experience invites me to new life.

This is most clearly seen in the experience of loving. This is not surprising, for loving is the essential activity, function, expression, of the human person. For the human person, to be alive is to be loving. Anything else is deadly.

To love demands I "let go" of my selfish concerns, my desire to control, my tendencies to manipulate, my fear of being known and rejected by others. Love demands a willingness to die to self. Love also demands a willingness to give, to be vulnerable, to share—and to have the hope that the other person will respond, so the love can become mutual.

Love is risky and dangerous. It takes a lot of dying, but it's the only way for humans to come alive. There is no rising without dying.

Fear of Dying

Life here, now—life to come. In the first fifty years of my life I did not understand, and certainly I did not experience, much connection between this life and the life to come.

My fear of death was rooted in this chasm between life here and now and the life to come. I was quite aware of being a sinner, of my sinful deeds. This was stressed over and over in all kinds of ways in school, in church, in religious books and in practices such as examinations of conscience and confession.

This awareness of being sinner made me fear judgment and, even more, death. I never felt sure my sins were forgiven...I mean really forgiven. I didn't want to think about dying. I was afraid to die.

One of the reasons for this fear of judgment and death lay in the emphasis on sin without a corresponding emphasis on God's mercy and forgiveness. As a result I knew I was a sinner; I did not realize I was also a holy person because of God's forgiveness.

With joy I have become more aware of the power of the

resurrection of Jesus in my daily life. This means that there is an important, inherent and ongoing relation between the here and now and the life to come.

Now, I hear anew Saint Paul's words: "We are afflicted in every way, but not constrained; perplexed, but not driven to despair; persecuted, but not abandoned; struck down, but not destroyed; always carrying about in the body the dying of Jesus, so that the life of Jesus may also be manifested in our body" (2 Corinthians 4:8-11; see also Romans 8:18-25).

Every moment of my daily life takes on meaning in light of the mystery of Jesus, especially his death and resurrection. All my experience is important not only in terms of life here and now, but also the life to come. The power of the risen Lord is at work in me here and now. My future and final resurrection is already beginning to happen now.

Christmas—Parousia. Another reason I fear death lies in the way I separate Christmas from the Parousia (Second Coming). We might not be familiar with the word *Parousia*, but we are all aware that "Jesus will come again to judge the living and the dead." That's what we say every Sunday in the Creed. That's what Parousia means. Most of us think that has nothing to do with Christmas!

But it does. I can't understand the Second Coming if I don't understand the first coming. I can't understand Jesus as our judge unless I understand the mystery of Christmas. The Second Coming is the fulfillment of the first; the first coming of Jesus in the flesh reaches its fulfillment only when Jesus comes in glory.

I'm not afraid of the Jesus wrapped in swaddling clothes and lying in a manger. Why am I so afraid of Jesus who is coming in glory? Jesus came at Christmas to be our savior. Jesus came in the flesh to share our human condition and show us how to live. Jesus's love reaches out to every one of us in a tender and strong way to heal and forgive, to encourage and challenge, to enliven and fulfill. Jesus is our Savior.

So, if we want to understand the Parousia, we must see it in light of Christmas. The Parousia is the fullness of Christmas. The Jesus who comes as a helpless, tiny baby is the Jesus who loves us, died for us, is risen for us. This is the Jesus who lives in us and walks with us every step of our way in daily life. This is the Jesus who, through his Spirit, empowers us—little by little, more and more—"to act justly, to love tenderly, and walk humbly with our God" (Micah 6:8). Christmas becomes Parousia!

Justice—mercy. I fear death; I fear being punished for sin after I die, I fear Jesus who will come to judge me when I die. Another reason such fear grips me lies in the way I separate God's justice and mercy.

There are lots of ways this happens. I used to think that the present time is a time of mercy, but when I die, I get justice. The time of mercy is over! I forget that the time for both justice and mercy is now!

I am aware that in this life the power of evil wars against the power of good. This struggle goes on in my heart, relationships, family, society, Church. It is also at work in the systems and structures of our society. Saint Paul portrays this struggle graphically (see Romans 7).

So, I am in a life-death struggle; I am on trial. My future is at stake. "What a person sows, he or she will reap." I will be held accountable for my deeds. There's no escaping this accountability; it's the burden of freedom. When I recall this I can lose heart. I can give up. Then I will indeed fear dying. I will fear Jesus "who comes to judge the living and the dead."

But, as we saw in the words of Paul, nothing "...will be able to separate us from the love of God in Christ Jesus our Lord" (Romans 8:39). This is the same Paul who said earlier, "...where sin increased, grace overflowed all the more" (Romans 5:20).

In God, in Jesus, justice and mercy are united as one. God's justice means he is true to himself as God of the covenant, the God of the Promise, the God who loves sinners, who calls sinners to forgiveness and life. God's justice means forgiveness to sinners (That's mercy!). God's mercy forgives sinners and reconciles them to God (That's justice!). Again, as Paul puts it: "For there is no distinction; all have sinned and are deprived of the glory of God. They are justified freely by his grace through the redemption in Christ Jesus..." (Romans 3:22-24). Sounds complicated, but it's simple: God loves sinners!

In light of this incredible Good News of God's merciful justice and justifying mercy, there is hope for us sinners. We can face judgment with confidence. There is every reason for us to trust in God's faithful and justifying love, to hope in God's merciful justice.

Love is stronger than death. Another aspect of my fear of death lies in my failure to "practice the truth in love." I don't love others enough. I don't practice the hard and difficult love of helping others face death.

I'm afraid to talk about dying. How often when someone is seriously ill, in danger of dying, I say things such as, "Don't worry. Everything will be all right." "You'll be back on your feet in no time." "Before you know it, you'll be as good as new." I do not practice the truth in love. We do not practice the truth! I try to bring comfort and cheer by hiding the truth, denying the truth.

From my faith I draw the strength to look death in the face, to open myself and accept being vulnerable. My faith gives us the power to open my arms to mortality, to embrace sister death as Saint Francis did. Faith enables us to approach death not cringing in abject fear, but in joyful and peaceful hope.

I need others throughout life. I need others especially when I approach death, my supreme birthday. I need to talk about dying not only when I'm on my deathbed, but also while I'm still healthy. This is not morbid. This is love that practices the truth.

I can find all kinds of moments for this kind of sharing and encouragement. Whenever there is a death in the family or among our friends and neighbors, I have a chance to talk about the meaning of dying. I need to comfort others by sharing my fears, anxieties and worries about my own dying. I can do this also by trying to help children and teenagers understand the Christian meaning of dying.

In a special and urgent way I need to talk about my dying in practical terms. I need to make practical preparations for dying. Often people will take pains to get a cemetery plot and put away money for casket and funeral, but little else. We hear a lot today about living wills, and rightly so! I need to talk about and make provisions for those times when I might not be able to speak for myself or make my wishes known.

Some families are torn to pieces because this kind of love and sharing was avoided. When a crisis came, it was too late. At a time when we need to be united in love and care and concern, we are torn apart by disagreements and arguments and hard feelings. Should the respirator be discontinued on a ninety-year-old mother? Should she ever be put on the respirator? Should a person undergo heart surgery at age eighty?

Endless and complex situations can arise, often suddenly and when we least expect. Each person is unique, and each has to face these questions in different ways. What is right and good for one may not be good for someone else. But we need to share our feelings and ideas on these matters while there's time, not when the pressure is on us.

The marvelous thing about "practicing the truth in love," especially on matters concerning death and dying, is that it not only flows from love, it deepens our love. It brings us closer together.

A final note: Grief and the pain of loss are always present when someone close dies. The separation of death calls forth deep feelings of anger, frustration, fear, anxieties. It calls forth deep eruptions of pain, sadness and the loneliness of a broken heart. Grieve we must, even shed tears. And it will go on for months!

But it is precisely in the midst of all this grief that our faith emerges and sustains us. Someone I love, someone I care so deeply about, someone for whom I want only the best—that someone has made it! There is so much reason for joy! The one I love is safe, at home, now fully alive, no more sorrow, no more pain, no more heartbreak.

It dawns on me that I must rejoice, sing, shout for joy, raise alleluias, for the one I love is now fully alive...and is waiting for me.

Indeed, perfect love casts out fear!

Today Is Resurrection Day

Our faith is full of paradoxes. It is marked by the Sign of the Cross. I am empowered by the Spirit to believe, to hope even when all the evidence is to the contrary. All the moments of daily living are marked not only by dying, but also by our rising to newness of life. The movement may not be very evident. I may not feel it. But it's real. Jesus has guaranteed it. I believe!

In a way Saint Paul sums it all up for us. He writes:

> We are afflicted in every way, but not constrained; perplexed, but not driven to despair; persecuted, but not abandoned; struck down, but not destroyed; always carrying about in the body the dying of Jesus, so that the life of Jesus may also be manifested in our body. For we who live are constantly being given up to death for the sake of Jesus, so that the life of Jesus may be manifested in our mortal flesh.... Therefore, we are not discouraged; rather, although our outer self is wasting away, our inner self is being renewed day by day. For this momentary light affliction is producing for us an eternal weight of glory, beyond all comparison. (2 Corinthians 4:8-11, 16-17)